REFORM

THE CHURCH AT THE BIRTH OF PROTESTANTISM

LUKE H. DAVIS

CF4•K

10 9 8 7 6 5 4 3 2

Reprinted in 2024
Paperback ISBN: 978-1-5271-0990-2
Ebook ISBN: 978-1-5271-1037-3

Published by Christian Focus Publications,
Geanies House, Fearn, Tain, Ross-shire,
IV20 1TW, Scotland, U.K.
www.christianfocus.com;
email: info@christianfocus.com

Design and illustrations: Laura K. Sayers
Cover designer: Catriona Mackenzie

Printed and bound in Malaysia

CONTENTS

DEDICATED TO

Rev. Dr. Ben Wagner,
Rector of the Anglican Church of the Resurrection,
Chesterfield, Missouri,

for guiding me through holy orders,
for giving me encouragement in darkness,
and for granting me renewed hope in Christ's Church.

Thank you for being a most blessed friend.

Begun over five hundred years ago in Germany, the ideas of the Protestant Reformation spread like wildfire, sweeping over many parts of Europe. The Reformation was like wildfire in another sense – it destroyed much of what had been before. The unity of European Christendom was dissolved, as was the uncontested authority of the Roman Catholic Church. But as Luke Davis conveys in *Reform: The Church in the Birth of Protestantism,* the fire of the Reformation was necessary to clear the ground for the biblical gospel to grow and blossom throughout the sixteenth century and beyond.

Readers of *Reform* will certainly learn why the Reformation is so important to the history of Christianity. But thanks to Davis's gift for bringing historical figures to life in vivid color and captivating details, readers will enjoy getting to know who the major and minor players were in this movement. These are not airbrushed portraits of saints we cannot relate to, however. Davis shows how the Reformers struggled with anxiety, fear, and had to endure hardship. And there were differences among some Reformers about how the Reformation should take shape. But Davis's vignettes show that what the Reformers had in common was a commitment to knowing the scripture and making it known, a compulsion to point people to Christ alone for salvation, and a willingness to suffer for the truth. Teen readers and readers of all ages should be inspired to follow in their footsteps. Perhaps God, in his mercy, will use the ideas and inspiration in this book to fan the flames of gospel revival in our generation?

Ben Wagner
Rector, Anglican Church of the Resurrection,
Chesterfield, Missouri

The Reformation was a pivotal point in church history, and Davis introduces us to the people who were there. There are engaging portraits of well-known names like Martin Luther and John Calvin as well as lesser known people, all going about the business of reforming the church. This book is rich in characters and theology, and is an enlightening read for teens.

Linda Finlayson
Author of *God's Timeline* and *God's Bible Timeline*

Luke Davis has given a human face to the Reformation, the most decisive event in Western church history in the past thousand years. Here you can read about the great heroes of the Protestant faith through whom God wrought His wonders in the 16th century. Hopefully it whets your appetite for further study. An excellent introduction!

Dr Nick Needham
Church History tutor, Highland Theological College,
Dingwall, Scotland

IMPORTANT MOMENTS IN THE REFORMATION ERA

c. 1450

Johannes Gutenberg invents his movable type printing press

1485

The Battle of Bosworth Field ends the War of the Roses

1492

Christopher Columbus discovers the New World

1498

Leonardo da Vinci finishes painting *The Last Supper*

1509

Desiderius Erasmus writes his satirical work, *In Praise of Folly*

1512

Michelangelo finishes painting the ceiling of the Sistine Chapel

1517

Martin Luther fastens his Ninety-Five Theses to Castle Church's door

1520

Jacques Lefèvre d'Étaples leaves Paris and escapes to Meaux

1521

Luther defends his teachings at the Imperial Diet in Worms

1523

Martin Bucer arrives in Strasbourg

1528

Patrick Hamilton is burned at the stake in St. Andrews, Scotland

1528

Balthasar Hubmaier is burned at the stake in Vienna

1530

The Augsburg Confession is accepted by Charles V

1531

Marguerite de Navarre writes "The Mirror of the Sinful Soul" poem

1533

Thomas Cranmer is appointed Archbishop of Canterbury

1534

Parliament passes the English Act of Supremacy

1536

William Tyndale is burned at the stake near Vilvoorde (near Brussels)

1538

John Calvin and William Farel are expelled from Geneva

1539

Printing of the English Bible

1541

John Calvin returns to Geneva from Strasbourg

1543

Catherine Parr marries King Henry VIII

1546

George Wishart is burned at the stake in St. Andrews, Scotland

1554

Lady Jane Grey is beheaded in the Tower of London

1555-56

Hugh Latimer, Nicholas Ridley, and Thomas Cranmer are martyred

1556

The women known as the Guernsey Martyrs are burned together

1558

Elizabeth I becomes Queen of England, re-establishes Protestantism

1559

John Calvin founds the Geneva Academy

1560

John Knox's *Scots Confession* is approved

1563

John Knox confronts Mary of Scots, regarding her proposed marriage

1571

The Thirty-Nine Articles of the Church of England are finalized

THE PROTESTANT REFORMATION

When my father was young, he lived in western Pennsylvania in the United States. One day, in the middle of the afternoon, the sky grew excessively dark. This wasn't a passing storm cloud. The middle of the afternoon looked like the beginnings of night! (In truth, a lot of soot blew down from Canada and covered the atmosphere in my father's region) The people there were alarmed by it, but they couldn't really do much about it. They knew though, that this was not the way the middle of the afternoon was supposed to look.

A parallel situation occurred in the late Middle Ages in Europe. Over time, the world grew dark. This wasn't a physical darkness, but a spiritual darkness. Many in the Christian lands of Europe were alarmed by what was going on, but not many of them knew what to do about it. There were a number, though, who instinctively came to realize that this was not how spiritual faith should look.

It was out of this increasing anxiety and determination that the Protestant Reformation was born. Now, those two words deserve further clarification. When we speak of *Protestant*, that is a name that both tells what one is *not* and what one *is*. Protestants (today this would include Anglicans, Episcopalians, Presbyterians, Baptists, Methodists, Congregationalists, and a host of other groups) do not belong to either the Roman Catholic or Eastern Orthodox faiths. But the word "Protestant" also displays something of who they are, believers who initially **protested** against the spiritual and moral decay they claimed had sabotaged the Roman Catholic Church. As a result, instead of merely complaining about these problems, they wished to **reform** the church, to call it back to its original teachings and vision found in the Bible and centered upon the completed work of Jesus Christ.

What were these concerns that the Protestant Reformation sought to address? Well, there were moral deficiencies that had grown amongst the Catholic faith over the Middle Ages. Sadly, a number of the Catholic **clergy** (ministers like priests, bishops, and popes) both exhibited immorality and benefited from the corruption in the church. Some priests could be named bishops (in fact, some men were named bishops before they had even been ordained as priests!) of a region or territory, and then they would never visit or be resident in that area. This **absenteeism** would help the bishops profit from money and offerings given to the churches in the region, but they were hardly doing their assigned work. In some cases, someone who wished to have the power and prestige of a church position (sometimes called "ecclesiastical office") and was wealthy enough could make a financial offer to a bishop, archbishop, or even a pope! After the monetary transaction, the clergyman would grant the payer a position within the church, even though he had not earned it through spiritual discipline or theological and biblical study. This practice—known as **simony** (named after Simon Magnus in the eighth chapter of Acts who attempted to purchase the power of the Holy Spirit from the apostle Peter)—became somewhat common in the medieval church. People who spoke out against this corruption could expect danger. One monk, Adam of Genoa, was murdered in bed in 1494 soon after he preached against simony. Monasteries faltered in their spiritual discipline and became centers of leisure and wealth. And though all clergy in the Catholic Church took a vow of celibacy, a number of them broke this vow, whether secretly or shamelessly. Even popes such as

Alexander VI (1431-1503; became pope in 1492) fathered several illegitimate children with a number of mistresses. With the corruption in the church, many people found it difficult to accept their ministers as men of God, unable to trust leaders who flaunted their own sin. Many priests who did take their vocation seriously found their honest labors to be overlooked or scorned.

But the moral failures of the church were only part of the equation. There were theological problems as well, regarding what the church taught about human salvation. What had developed over the course of the Middle Ages was an increasingly complex path called the *sacramental system*. One should realize that at their core, sacraments (i.e. baptism and Holy Communion[1]) are essential actions that Jesus confirmed as activities His followers should partake of. What had occurred in the medieval church was that the number of sacraments had mushroomed to a total of seven[2] and had become a working list by which one gauged their salvation. In the sacramental system of the medieval church, baptism would wash away one's sin from birth, but one would still sin and so this is where other sacraments (particularly Communion and confession) came into play. Having faith in Christ would justify the medieval believer[3], but then the person's sinful actions would bring about God's displeasure, so to maintain a proper level of God's grace in one's life, you would need to go to Communion and receive an infusion of God's mercy by your participation. You would also need to go and confess your sins to a priest, who might give you "homework" in the form of certain prayers or actions to perform to demonstrate your sincerity. Where this led was that the sacraments were no longer for

---

1. Sometimes called the Lord's Supper or the Eucharist; Catholics referred to a service of Holy Communion as the Mass.
2. Those seven being baptism, Holy Communion, confirmation (of one's faith), confession/ penance, holy orders (priest ordination), marriage, and last rites.
3. That is, make the believer initially accepted in God's sight.

encouraging God's people and strengthening their faith[4], but rather exercises required to maintain an acceptable standing in God's eyes. They were not joyous occasions that Christians were able to do; they were labors that they were pressured to do. And from this, one could never be sure of God's love and acceptance. Churchgoers spiritually lived on the edge. And perhaps you might wonder, "Well, why didn't they just read the Bible to figure out what the truth was?" That actually was part of the problem. Many people in the Middle Ages were unable to read well, if at all, and those who could read their own language could have difficulty understanding the Bible, which was largely available only in the Latin translation going back to Jerome. The darkness of spiritual ignorance covered the skies of a lost Europe.

Into this wider community, the Reformers got to work. The spiritual light of the Protestant Reformation did not shine all at once, for some had already challenged the Roman Catholic consensus before (we have already mentioned some in the previous book, *Reign*, like John Wycliffe and John Hus), and it took time for the Protestant teachings to move throughout the nations of Europe. Additionally, the Reformers were not in lock-step on every single issue.[5] However, there were key areas where the great Protestant Reformers displayed incredible unity. These areas became known as the *solas* of the Reformation, referring to the Latin word "sola", meaning "alone."

The Reformers believed and taught the principle of *sola Scriptura*: Scripture alone. This did not mean that Christians should only read the Bible and ignore other works. Nor did the Reformers believe this meant that the Bible gave

4. See the Fact File chapter on the Reformers and worship for a general Protestant understanding of sacraments like Holy Communion.

5. For instance, Martin Luther and Ulrich Zwingli had sharp disagreement on what exactly happened to the bread and wine in Holy Communion. On the matter of church leadership, John Calvin believed in the role of pastors and elders, while English Reformers like Thomas Cranmer believed in the position of bishops.

fully authoritative answers to every specific situation one could face. Nor did the Reformers believe that the great tradition of how Christians had interpreted the Bible should be overthrown. What they *did mean* is that **Scripture is the supreme authority of Christian faith and activity.** Nothing outranks the Bible in terms of where it stands for the Christian. Scripture is absolutely and without question God's sufficient, powerful, satisfying, and completely authoritative revelation about Himself, centered on Jesus Christ, and understood by the power of the Holy Spirit. And because it was so essential that Scripture be understood by ordinary Christians, the Reformers also believed that the Bible should be translated into the common language of people and preached faithfully to them in their language.

The early Protestant leaders also cherished that human salvation was conferred by *sola gratia*: grace alone. While sin has separated us from God, all is not lost! But for the story to have a happy ending, God must write the story of our salvation. He saves us from our rebellion against Him and waywardness from Him, not because He sees our sincerity or our determination to do good things or because He sees some spiritual potential in us. The Reformers noted Paul's words in Romans 5:8 that "God shows His love for us in that *while we were still sinners,* Christ died for us." We bring nothing to the table for our salvation, no good résumé, no bargaining chip. God offers His grace, for the simple reason that He wants to do so. He simply desires to show His incredible compassion to sinful people!

But what makes the connection between us and God? It would be *sola fide*: faith alone. Here we need to be careful and define faith, because this does not mean having faith that you might win the lottery or have faith that Manchester United will win the Premier League. Christian faith means that the only way we receive God's grace is by placing our trust in Jesus Christ. We in effect say "I am putting myself completely in Jesus' hands, fully relying on Him for what He did in dying on the cross, because He suffered the penalty that I deserved for my sin. And I trust in His resurrection, because He shattered the grip that sin had on me." Do you see what faith does? We are admitting that we have to place our trust in someone outside of ourselves: Jesus Christ. What saves us is only faith, the complete opposite of pridefully depending upon ourselves. And this is a faith that doesn't stay at the starting line, but grows. John Calvin noted that "it is faith alone which justifies, and yet the faith which justifies is not alone." Thomas Cranmer of the English Reformation wrote that saving faith "does not lie dead in the heart, but is lively and fruitful."[6]

The aspect of faith in Jesus Christ leads us to consider the fourth "sola" of the Reformers, *solus Christus*: Christ alone. The grace of God leads us to faith which we place only in Christ. This is because only Jesus could be the one who could accomplish our salvation. Human beings are sinful and separated from God, but this is a situation which we have brought on ourselves and are responsible to deal with as humans. But because of our sin and separation from God, we don't have the ability to save ourselves. So, we require someone who can represent us before God as a human being, but also do so in moral and spiritual perfection as God. Jesus Christ is the only One who can do that, noted the Reformers. Martin Luther loved passages that showed this, like I Timothy 2:5, "For there is one God, and there is *one mediator* between God and men, the man Christ Jesus." No one else could be the recipient of our faith but Jesus. No one else could accomplish salvation for us but Jesus.

Finally, the Reformers believed that all of life should be lived *soli Deo gloria*: to the glory of God alone. Our existence is meant to be a journey on which our words, actions, and

6. The Reformers would have believed this was a logical extension of II Corinthians 5:17: "Therefore, if anyone is in Christ, he is a new creation. The old has passed away; behold, the new has come."

attitudes point others, not to ourselves, but to God. This is something that, of course, we will be seeking to make more and more a reality throughout our lives. But a Christian saved by grace and exhibiting a lively faith in Christ will desire to live a more God-focused and heaven-directed life. And this means asking ourselves, "What does God require of me?" rather than thinking first and foremost about our own desires. Our hearts are throne rooms, and for the Christian believer, God must sit on that throne.

Yes, the Protestant Reformation was a time of confrontation, hope, and rich variety. But most of all, it was a movement of the *solas*, each of which led into the next one. If we believe in *Scripture alone,* we see that we can only have hope in God's *grace alone*, which we receive through *faith alone* in *Christ alone*, and thus we can live to *the glory of God alone.*

All this from a powerful historical shift, after which the world would never be the same again.

FACT FILES

The Renaissance: The Foundation of the Reformation

Perhaps you have been in a neighborhood or along a busy road and you discover that a construction company is beginning the process of building one or several new homes. Or it could be a new place of business like a bank or restaurant. The workers are just starting their work, and in their initial activity, there is surely something they do *not* do! They will not get the lumber, dry wall, wiring and outlets, plumbing pipes or valves together and start putting together the house on the ground as it is! Well, they could, but it would be an insane idea. What is required first is to grade the ground and then install a *foundation* on which they might build. It could be a concrete slab, a crawlspace, or a full basement, but the workers have to labor and have a solid space upon which they might construct the building. Without the foundation, the building will struggle to stand.

In a way, the period known as the Renaissance served as a foundation for the construction of the Protestant Reformation. As the Middle Ages drew to a close, a great deal of creative energy began to flow throughout Europe. Historians have named this time period (roughly the fifteenth and sixteenth centuries) the *Renaissance* because the word refers to a sense of renewal, of rebirth, or a re-captured approach to the flourishing of life.

There were several ingredients to the Renaissance. One in particular was its location; although it affected many parts of Europe, the center of Renaissance activity was Italy. Florence was the city often viewed as the epicenter of the movement, with other cities like Genoa, Venice, Milan, Bologna, and Rome playing large supporting roles. But the most essential elements of the Renaissance were the values and commitments of what made life worth living.

Humanism was at the center of the Renaissance. At this point, this did not mean exalting people and ignoring God. The humanism of the Renaissance was a conviction that human beings were principally important in the establishing of civilization. When life was made more grand and glorious, humankind was at the forefront of that movement. So the study of human action and creation was front and center during the Renaissance. The learning of Latin to understand classical texts also helped educated people understand their own traditions and languages better, and the urgency of the day was to return to the classical, ancient sources of virtue and truth. "Ad fontes!", or "To the sources!" was a rallying cry. Artistic creativity and expression increased greatly in many disciplines: in painting with an application of linear perspective, light, and shadow; in sculpture with a focus on human form and dignity; and in architecture with a passion for beauty and order in columns, arches, and pilasters. Thinkers pursued the methods of science, asking probing questions and making new discoveries about the structure of the universe, the features of human anatomy, plant life, acoustics, and medicine. Others reasoned that humans could make new discoveries in geography, and a new age of exploration began as sailors encountered new lands and cultures half a world away. Music evolved into a richer discipline in the Renaissance with the development of polyphony (at least two lines of melody), triadic harmony (three-note chords), and the use of vocal music to express the desires of the human spirit.

It was in this context that the Reformation was born. While there are many people in the Renaissance who made impact that benefited the coming Reformation, four in particular are worth mentioning specifically.

Leonardo da Vinci (1452-1519) is considered one of the ideal "Renaissance men." Famous as an artist, da Vinci's interests ranged into many disciplines, including architecture, anatomy, botany, and others. His notebooks bear his drawings and comments on a wide variety of subjects. The most famous of his paintings, *The Mona Lisa*, hangs in the Louvre in Paris. His *Vitruvian Man* drawing exhibits what he believed to be ideal human body proportions. And his most stunning religious artwork, ***The Last Supper***, is a masterpiece of human emotion, use of space and light, and the focal point of Jesus' face. It is still the most reproduced piece of religious art in world history, a fact which obscures a subtle message of the work, that Jesus' word and action are so focal we must find our place in our reaction to Him. As da Vinci was completing the painting, his friend Luca Pacioli declared it to be "a symbol of man's burning desire for salvation." Given that human salvation was the keystone of the Reformation, da Vinci's work sets a proper foundation for such matters.

With the intellectual ferment leading to a greater desire to read, the market for published books was greater than ever. Yet prior to the Renaissance, the printing of books was a high-labor activity and an expensive manner of production. Perhaps monks would copy books by hand on paper in the monastery scriptorium. Or those who worked as printmakers would make texts based on carved wooden blocks set to reproduce each page. So, each page would require a new block. Whether one was a monk or a printmaker, the technique was lengthy and difficult. Producing one small book could take about six months! All this changed around 1450 when the German printer ***Johannes Gutenberg*** invented the first movable type printing press from his shop in Mainz. Using individual metal pieces called *matrices*, Gutenberg was able to place them in a larger block pattern and—using oil-based inks that made a cleaner copy—make copies of pages that way. When he needed to print a new page, he could rearrange the matrices to reflect the text and produce more copies in quicker fashion. The number of published copies produced in Europe rose from practically nothing to ten million copies after Gutenberg produced his press, and to **two hundred million copies during the sixteenth century** as more presses were constructed! Of particular note is how this invention quickened the spread of knowledge and information in the Renaissance. Also, the accessibility to Scripture (an essential desire of the Reformers) was heightened by Gutenberg's work: The first book he printed on his movable type press was the Bible.

The work of artist and sculptor ***Michelangelo*** (1475-1564) brought the vividness of biblical characters and scenes into the human mind and imagination. This Italian was commissioned by the Roman Catholic Church to produce great works to draw the human spirit heavenward in awe. At twenty-four years of age, he carved the *Pieta* (a sculpture depicting the grieving Mary holding the lifeless body of the crucified Jesus as she holds him in her lap) from a single block of marble. In his hometown of Florence, Michelangelo then fashioned his most famous statue, *David*, a carved masterwork of Carrara marble that displayed the king of ancient Israel in unclothed glory, showing the technical skill of the young artist who was concerned to show the beauty of God's creatures. Yet his most demanding work might have been his painting in the Sistine Chapel in the Vatican (the same room where the leaders of the Catholic Church vote for a new pope when required). From 1508 to 1512, Michelangelo would ascend to the scaffold, lie on his back, and paint biblical scenes on the sections of the barrel-vaulted ceiling. On the side panels, he painted men and women from Scripture and history prophesying the arrival of Christ, while in the center of the ceiling, he painted nine pictures from the Book of Genesis, from the event of creation to the Great Flood.

Michelangelo's work breathed new life into the beauty of Scripture in the years preceding the Reformation. What is lesser known about Michelangelo is that he was an outstanding poet, as well. As the Reformation made advances into Italy, the artist developed a deepening friendship with a woman, Vittoria Colonna, who was a devout believer in the Gospel proclaimed by the Reformers. Her influence led the introspective Michelangelo to consider the grace of God's salvation that was so evident in his artwork all along. One of his last paintings was *The Last Judgment*, in which Michelangelo depicted himself standing before Christ, sinful and in full need of the grace of Jesus. Twinned with this view of himself are these words from one of Michelangelo's sonnets, a fervent reflection that Jesus alone was his only hope:

The thorns and nails and both your palms,
together with your kind, humble, merciful face;
promise to the sinful soul the grace
of deep repentance and hope of salvation.
May your holy eyes and pure ears
not respond with rigorous justice to my past life;
may your severe arm not stretch out towards it.
May your blood alone cleanse and remove my sins;
and may it more abound the older I am,
with ready help and with complete forgiveness.

Finally, the work of ***Desiderius Erasmus*** (1466-1536) might have opened the door to the Protestant Reformation more than any other person. This Dutch humanist and Catholic priest wrote more than two hundred books in his lifetime, and his passion was calling people away from spiritual wandering and back to true religion. His favorite activities were studying the Greek language, reading the New Testament (in the original Greek) and early leaders of the ancient Church, and reforming the ills of society. He demanded the Catholic Church return to taking the New Testament seriously and following Christ with full devotion, with Scripture as the supreme source of faith and daily life. He could write with biting sarcasm and satire. His *In Praise of Folly* ridiculed the abuses and corruption in the Catholic Church, laying a foundation for the Protestant Reformers to criticize Rome when they believed it had drifted from grace. Erasmus also wrote works like *Julius Excluded From Heaven*, in which he depicted the former Pope Julius II arriving at the gates of heaven after his death and being turned away from Paradise. But Erasmus was most effective with his demands to take Scripture seriously. He pressed the need to (a) use the Greek New Testament as a basis for study to understand God's true message, (b) interpret the Bible by considering the historical and literary context of what is written, and (c) the best way to raise enlightened Christians was to provide a humanist education in classical texts, languages, and the New Testament. His rallying cry was always, "To the sources!" Many of these principles were seized by the Reformers, especially Martin Luther. In fact, a number of people have said, "Erasmus laid the egg and Luther hatched it", when referring to the Reformation.

The Renaissance was not the Protestant Reformation, but the Reformation could not have advanced as it did unless the Renaissance came before it. And what is so striking is how the chief examples of the Renaissance used their gifts in that way. An artist and scientist like Leonardo da Vinci showed the bold color of God's story of salvation, a story that the Reformers made more clear. The printer Johannes Gutenberg provided the means by which the Word of God would have a principled place in the lives of

Christians. The sculptor, painter, and poet Michelangelo drew peoples' spirits to the beauty of biblical faith and the hope one can only have in Christ alone. And Desiderius Erasmus pushed open the door that brought fresh air to the precious Reformed teaching that Scripture, not human ideas, are our supreme guide for our faith.

JACQUES LEFÈVRE D'ÉTAPLES

June 1524; Meaux, France

Rain, thought Gerard as he squinted through the sheets pouring down from the heavens. *How odd that normally I hate it, but today it would cover up any tracks and movements.* He skirted past a cart of lowing cattle whose master drove them furiously through the mire. Looking down the street either way, Gerard was of two objectives: to find the man he needed, and to avoid the authorities who would seize him.

A shout from the west end of the market caught his attention, and Gerard saw a cluster of soldiers making their way down the street in the direction of the cheese factory. So taken was Gerard with their destination that his mouth began to water at the thought of the straw-colored, creamy delicacies, that he shuffled directly into the path of an unsuspecting passerby.

"I beg your pardon, my good man," said the figure, water splashing off the hood of his soaked cowl.

"Well, that's what comes of ..." Gerard began before he recognized the man. "Master Lefèvre!" he whispered, so as not to be overheard. "I've been looking for you! We must get you out of the open and hide you!"

"A good thought," said Lefèvre, his voice raspy and the rain dripping down his face as he lifted his hood. "Where did you have in mind?"

Gerard grunted at his own impertinence, but he grabbed the hood of Lefèvre's cloak and pulled it back over his head. "Not here in the open! Please, my friend, keep your head covered so they will not discover you here!"

"Who?" Lefèvre demanded.

Gerard put his finger to his lips, mouthing his next words slowly. "Not here. Quickly, to the bishop's quarters. Haven't you heard?"

"Of what?"

Gerard looked his friend in the eye. "The Sorbonne and the courts, sire. Their condemnation has been handed down. We need to see Briçonnet now!"

After slushing through puddles and falling once or twice in the heavy gale that caused the rain to sting their skin, the two arrived at the bishop's house, where a servant passed on a message they were to meet Bishop Briçonnet in the cathedral next door. "But he gave strict instructions," noted the servant, "that you both are to go around the church and enter by the south tower door."

"All the way around!" griped Gerard as they rounded the cathedral on the east side. "The north tower is practically next to the bishop's house! Why would he do this?"

"Peace, good Gerard," came the soothing voice of Jacques Lefèvre, as his foot skidded in a puddle, with only his sudden grip on the stony exterior of the cathedral saving him from falling. "Whatever the case, I am certain that he has his reasons."

Ascending the three steps to the door at the south tower, Gerard looked behind as Lefèvre joined him at the door. There was still enough light in the raging storm so a keen eye could view both of them. Just before he could mutter a further complaint about the bishop's plan, the great south door opened and a hand, thrust through the space between the door's edge and the frame, waved them in.

Willing their soaked bodies through the door, both Gerard and the inexplicably calm Lefèvre beheld one of the cathedral workers blinking at them in the gloom. "Welcome, both of you," he said, pointing up the stairs. "His Grace desires to meet you in the organ balcony. Take the stairs. I myself will come behind you with a towel to wipe your wet footprints."

"Is this the bishop's idea?" Gerard demanded, but Lefèvre interrupted him.

"If so, it is a good one." He nodded to the worker, clad in a gray cloak, "Thank you, friend. We will trust you to do as you say. Gerard, with me." And he led the way up the stairs.

The balcony was shrouded in darkness, and both men strained their eyes to see any movement. Finally, a form glided out behind a pillar. "Brothers, you have come."

"Indeed, Your Grace," Lefèvre addressed Guillame Briçonnet, the bishop of Meaux. "I believe that any reason for this summons is absolutely urgent?"

"More than you know," said the bishop, "and really, Jacques, we've known each other long enough that in private moments like these, you can just call me Guillame."

"The habit is too rigidly formed, Your Grace," Lefèvre smiled.

"His politeness does him credit," Gerard said, anxious for notice.

Briçonnet gave the slightest of nods. "I assume that you were followed by my assistant who removed as much evidence of your entry as possible?"

"Indeed, Your Grace," said Lefèvre, "we are grateful for his work, aren't we, Gerard?"

"Absolutely," Gerard mumbled, now realizing the strategy of the drying towel.

"Now," the bishop continued, looking down into the nave of the cathedral, "I wish to convey news at all speed. Jacques, do you know why I asked you here today?"

"Gerard did not inform me of your reasons," replied Lefèvre, "only that my presence was required as soon as possible."

"To say 'soon' doesn't do justice to what we require," the bishop grumbled in exasperated fashion. "Why else would I ask you here?"

"Regarding my publication?" asked Lefèvre.

"Your translation of the New Testament is merely a spark for a wildfire that is spreading throughout our land. You have done good and godly work, Jacques. To have God's Word in our hands and in our own language is what we must have in order to train our churchmen, understand the road of faith, and reform our church along moral grounds. For too long have we drunk from the well of corruption and manipulation to build the church of our Lord. And yes, I backed you in your desire to make Holy Scripture plain to anyone in our nation who can read. I am simply speaking to you today because boldness brings about consequences, and we must faithfully face those trials well."

"The trials you speak of, Your Grace," said Lefèvre unsteadily, "must be recent ones, for I have received no such word."

"That would be my intention," Briçonnet replied. "I want you to know that I do not do this to surprise you, and I did not intend to hoard information from you. I wanted to be sure of the news and I needed to have trusted sources. But the truth is that your French New Testament has made you an outcast."

"How do you mean?" Lefèvre asked, struggling to regain his composure.

"A messenger from Paris sped this way on horseback, and how he did so without his steed perishing, I do not know," the bishop replied, sitting down. "The learned doctors of the Sorbonne met just yesterday. They discussed your work at length, presumably to give the impression they were granting a fair hearing, but with one voice they declared that any Scriptures in the language of the people have no place within this Catholic nation."

"How can they declare that?" Gerard exclaimed, his volume overpowered by the clap of thunder from outside. "It is no different from what John Wycliffe did over a century ago in England! By heaven, he even translated from the Latin Scriptures of St. Jerome, just as Master Lefèvre has done. Why is the church refusing to acclaim his work?"

"Something about your tone, Your Grace, tells me it is not merely the doctors of the church who are resisting," offered Lefèvre, the wrinkles in his face bunching with sad anticipation for what was to come.

Briçonnet nodded slowly, and his face fell. "Indeed, Jacques. The courts of law throughout Paris have laid down a criminal edict against your translation. This means that wherever your work is found, it is to be turned over to the authorities and burned."

"Savages!" Gerard spat.

"Gerard, peace," Lefèvre cautioned his friend. "Anger will not help us."

"Our work here in Meaux, searching the Scriptures and the great sources of the ancient fathers ... all we do for the cause of learning in our community, and this is what happens?" Gerard was nearly beside himself.

"It is not the unleashing of knowledge the courts condemn, good Gerard," the bishop responded, rising from his seat as shouts became audible outside. "Jacques, does Gerard know about your additions to the Scriptures?"

Lefèvre hesitated. "Not additions to the Word of God itself, Your Grace." He turned to Gerard. "As part of my endeavor, I also extracted shorter versions of the Gospels and some of the Epistles. I believed the smaller editions would introduce more people to portions of the Scriptures and cause them to hunger for more of God's Word. In those works, I wrote a preface and also noted some of my musings about various passages, especially in the apostle's letter to the Romans."

"And what did you go public with?" Briçonnet urged him, knowing the answer.

Lefèvre spread his hands, palms up. "I said that our only true standard that can establish Christian doctrine is the Scripture itself. Not the church, nor councils, nor popes."

"And also?" continued the bishop.

"Gerard needs to know," Lefèvre uttered with a sigh, gesturing to his friend, "for he needs to understand what is required. I followed Paul's logic to the very end. If we are truly sinful, and if the wages of sin is indeed death, and if we only can have peace with God through the sacrifice of Jesus Christ, then it follows we are justified, we are granted acceptance by God solely by faith in the death of Christ."

"And the sacraments? Baptism? Confession? Confirmation? The Eucharist?" asked Gerard.

"A formative and necessary part of the Christian's journey of faith," Lefèvre said, "but not what justifies a believer. Faith alone does. Faith alone must."

For over a minute, no one said anything. Finally, the bishop broke the silence. "You see, Gerard, why we had to discuss this matter. It goes to the very heart of everything our circle had discussed, learned, taught, and prayed for the last three years since we gathered together."

Before either Lefèvre or Gerard could respond, the loud creaking of the south tower door turned their minds away from the matter at hand. Stormy words wafted up the stairway and Bishop Briçonnet began making toward the balcony door.

"Your Grace," Lefèvre implored him, "you do not know who has come?"

"I know Whose I am," the bishop replied, not even glancing at them, peeking through the doorway down the stairs, he raised a palm in their direction. "Wait here," he whispered, "and if you must talk, keep your voices at an absolute hush!"

"He's been downstairs for some time, Jacques," Gerard mouthed.

Lefèvre had been silent, keeping his head bowed in prayer, but he raised himself and turned to his friend. "Which means that whoever came is not up here, for which I believe we should give thanks."

"Jacques, why did the bishop mention our circle of friends?" Gerard asked him.

Here Lefèvre looked somewhat sad. "Circles come and go. Friends dwell together and then must bear their own parting. That seemed to be what the bishop indicated. This has an effect on our fellowship that has enjoyed so much together."

"But why? Surely the bishop supports your teachings? You don't believe he would betray you?"

"No, I have no worries of that, Gerard. But I seem to have wounded an angry beast in the Sorbonne doctors and the judges of the land. I seem to have created a worse storm than the one raging outside at the moment. The rage of the church at this time will make it untenable for us to remain here in Meaux. My words bear too much similarity to Luther's in Wittenberg. And Luther is correct when he speaks of faith as what justifies us before God. If the church will not accept that, I must accept the danger in which I find myself. But wait! I hope this is just the bishop ascending the stairs!"

It was. Bishop Briçonnet glided into the balcony and signaled they be at ease. "It was what I feared: A pack of soldiers from Paris. They seemed to be a group that came of their own accord. In a way, that is good. They did not come from the palace, and if that is the case, then perhaps King Francis can use his influence to shield you from harm. But if they are sent from other sources, they may have no desire to treat you kindly. I must insist that you, Jacques, consider leaving Meaux as soon as you can, and Gerard, you would be wise to do the same."

"One question, Your Grace," Levefre asked, "but how did you manage to turn those soldiers away from searching the cathedral?"

A slight grin flitted over the bishop's face. "I caused them to chase you elsewhere. They asked if you were here and demanded to take you under their protection."

"Protection!" sneered Gerard.

"And you said?" asked Lefèvre.

"I said I had only seen you once in the past week and they would be better seeking you in other locations."

"You lied?" Gerard blurted out, incredulous.

"His Grace did not lie," said Lefèvre. "In truth, he has seen me only once in the past week. It just happened to be today at this time. But he didn't need to tell my pursuers that." Lefèvre clasped the bishop's hand. "Thank you, Guillaume," he rasped, using the bishop's personal name, "I shall not forget your kindness."

"There is no need to thank me," Briçonnet said, "but you two should busy yourselves warning the rest of our friends."

"Francois and Charles we can find and warn them," Lefèvre assured him.

"And no need to find Farel," Gerard added. "He was headed toward the Dauphine[7] and mentioned going on to Switzerland. He's likely made it as far as Citeaux already." He trailed off, looking around the expanse of the cathedral. "It's sad, though. Our fellowship has done so much to edify me with the Scriptures and the truth of Christ. Now what will happen if we fracture and scatter?"

"A faithful God will see to our efforts," Briçonnet replied, laying his hand on Gerard's shoulder.

"Indeed," said Lefèvre, "our Lord will remain faithful to see this is not the end. Remember, both of you, how Paul and Barnabas divided when they couldn't agree. A sad

---

7. The Dauphine was a province in southeastern France.

moment, but consider how apart they could cover twice as much ground. Now God places before us a glorious opportunity. Instead of keeping the riches of His Gospel here in Meaux, we can bring the faith to wherever He shall send us!"

The French humanist and priest **JACQUES LEFÈVRE D'ÉTAPLES** (1455-1536) was a forerunner of the Protestant Reformation, diligently seeking the moral and theological transformation of the Catholic Church in France. A student of theology and philosophy in the Italian Renaissance, he became a professor at the University of Paris, where his students included William Farel, who would be a leader in the Swiss Reformation with John Calvin. Some of his students joined him at Meaux, just over thirty miles east of Paris, where they, along with Bishop Briçonnet, formed the *Circle of Meaux*, a reforming group serious about studying the Scriptures and reforming the church. Although Lefèvre died in 1536, his legacy continued in the spread of ideas that shaped early Protestantism and inspired the Reformed believers in France.

MARTIN LUTHER

April 18, 1521, Worms, Germany

The water was refreshing, but bitterly cold, thought the professor. Splashing it over his face and neck, he tried desperately to revive himself after a sleepless night on an unforgiving bed. His time before the imperial court yesterday had ended with him under the savage glare of his examiners, to whom he croaked a sheepish request after no words came in reply.

"Your Graces," Martin bleated then in a voice that did not match his stocky frame, "might I have more time to consider my answer?"

He could sense rather than hear the disappointed sighs from the crowd behind him. A number of them had been in the vocal throng that flocked around Martin when he rode into the imperial city of Worms the preceding afternoon, and given the rumors flying about the city from that point on, everyone was expecting a titanic clash of wills between Luther and the representative of the church. Nothing short of a verbal bloodbath would satisfy the onlookers who counted themselves fortunate to secure a seat inside the great hall of the Heylshof Garden.

The presiding officer, Eck, scowled with frustration at Martin's balking words. Clear that he desired an immediate reply, Eck stepped in front of Martin so closely that the professor could smell what he had consumed for lunch that day. *Roasted goose and sour cabbage*, thought Martin, the very smell sending his belly into convulsions.

"More time?" Eck wheedled, making especially sure to drench his words in a sneer. "We have given you months, and you request even *more* time?"

Martin's friend and legal ally, Jerome Schruff, drew to his side. "You have placed twenty-five books in front of my friend, Master Eck. There is much here on this table before us to consider. Surely there is no trouble in appointing a brief respite for consideration, and Master Luther shall give you a definitive answer."

Eck looked back at the papal delegation arranged at the front of the room. One of the legates slyly nodded and raised his index finger barely an inch off his right thigh. Eck wheeled around and glared at Luther.

"We will grant you a full day's time," he growled, "and you shall appear before this court and give us a full and clear reply, four hours after midday tomorrow!"

"We thank you," Schruff said, bowing, before steering Martin away from the table as the crowd within the hall murmured in confusion. "And Martin," he whispered, "for your sake and for our city, I pray that your reply will be full and clear indeed."

Martin could only look back at Eck's glare. He and Eck had once been good friends, but three years ago that warmth had disappeared. *How could I have imagined, he thought, that fastening my words to the church door would have unleashed all of this?*

As he slept fitfully, Martin kept returning in his mind's eye to that day, that morning when everything had changed forever. Leaving his house with determined, yet trembling steps, the moisture from his palm seemed as if it would soak the paper rolled up in his hand. Every step he took, he believed his knees would give way and send him crashing to the ground. Although he had drunk a small pitcher of water before he swept through the front door of his house, his mouth felt as dry as a drought-wracked grass field.

How could I have been so bold in writing what I believe to be true, he asked himself, and now I am wondering what will come? For me? For any who believe in what I say?

Shuffling along toward the dark spire of Castle Church, Martin briefly unrolled the paper once more, reading as his pace quickened. His words—no doubt they were his words—lay on the page in his forceful script that pled with the church to stop what it was doing. Are the certificates known as indulgences, the proof of payment to the church authorities, to be taken seriously as the purchase of forgiveness of sins? Those who preach in favor of these indulgences, he shook his head, are in error when they say people are forgiven every penalty of sin and are saved by purchase of these measly scraps of paper. Martin smiled ruefully, remembering writing those words just a few days ago. *That was number twenty-one*, he recalled.

Past the public house, past the linen peddler's shop, and on he went, his pace now rapid like his breathing. It was All Hallows' Eve, he told himself, the thirty-first day of October, and so many people would be making their way to the church for services. *You have nothing to fear*, Martin told himself. *You just want to discuss these matters. This is a conversation with the church you love. And besides, who in town will be able to read these all the way through?*

He did not know how long he'd been standing at the door of the church, only that he'd traversed the distance there. Closing his eyes and then re-opening them, Martin looked down at the paper he held in his hands. His words. His handwriting. He thanked God he'd written it in Latin. It didn't do any good to involve a wider group of citizens of his town. The Roman Church would listen to reason, wouldn't they?

He saw the hammer lying at the base of the church door. Leaning down, Martin grasped it firmly in his right hand and positioned the paper with his protestations—all ninety-five of them—on the wooden door.

Thwack! Thwack! Thwack!

The paper was attached to the door. His journey that day was over.

What Martin could not imagine was that a new journey was about to begin.

The chatter and clamor in the hall of the Heylshof Garden drowned out Martin's ability to hear what Eck was uttering to his compatriots. As the prosecutor turned back toward the table piled with books, he called for silence and motioned for Martin to rise and face him.

"We have graciously afforded you a full day to weigh your response, Master Luther, and to give it full understanding before you share your reasons with us," Eck's words peppered the air with their strength. "Are you ready to give your statement in response to our questions?"

Martin placed his hands at his side and nodded ever so slightly to Eck and, behind him, the other dignitaries. "I am."

Eck swept his cloak around dramatically. "Then we shall hear it. But it is only fair that we should give you solemn warning that for you to return to the arms of Holy Mother Church, all you say will only grant you hope and reprieve if you end on one word. *Revoco*, I recant all."

This is it, Martin thought, casting a sideways glance at his ruler and benefactor, Frederick the Wise. The Duke of Saxony sat with a focused yet kindly look. He was leafing through several pages in his hands as he nodded encouragingly to Martin. *Does he really see the path I am about to take?* Martin told himself. *The easy way is to return to Rome, the difficult path to tread is God's truth. How many times did the apostles and martyrs of years past have to choose between security and faithfulness? Why do you, O God, lay this burden on me?*

"Martin Luther!" Eck snapped. "Are you willing to answer or are you not?"

Clasping his hands in front of him and gulping hard, Martin nodded again. "Yes, sire."

"Then may we have your response so that we might get on," groused the weary Emperor Charles from his throne, bringing scattering agreements from the crowd.

"I beg your pardon" Martin said, swallowing again, "but what I desire to say now is of utmost importance." He looked down at the paper with the word *revoco* next to the place for his signature. *Give me courage, Lord Christ,* he prayed.

He continued, "This shall be my word of defense. First, I desire to confess the wrongdoing of my manners. I am a blunt person, and I am afraid my training in law from years past has not granted me an even-handed temper when writing forth my convictions. I am plain and direct, not elegant of speech. Some of this will show up in my writings."

"So, you confess they are yours?" shouted Eck.

"Yes, all these books are mine," Luther calmly replied, his eyes locked with Eck's. "But it is unfair to restrict them to one category. Some of them are works of the history of the church, of philosophical discussions, and these writings are ones in which even my opponents today recognize their worth."

"You shall not delay our judgment!" sneered one of the priests seated near the emperor. "Little monk, it is a dangerous path you tread now!"

As if he hadn't heard the priest's volley, Martin kept speaking aloud. "There are books here in which I attack the falsehoods of the church past and present." He paused as the rumbles of assent and protest both grew louder from the assembly. "The obscuring and denial of the grace of God found in Jesus Christ, the proclamation and defense of indulgences, and the wrongful declarations of the pope himself are wounds to the flock of the Good Shepherd which I shall never ignore, and neither can the people of God unless they wish their own peril! I cannot and will not reject these writings unless I desire to uphold the very spiritual abuses and vile teachings they criticize. To recant my inscriptions would be to open wide the door to further deception on the part of those who claim to be the representatives of Christ on earth! And I will not strengthen such tyranny against the Gospel of the Lord!"

"You have condemned yourself!" growled the emperor, earning a doting nod from Eck.

"I shall ignore that interruption and speak to my third group of books," said Martin. "In these, I do speak against the teachings of individuals that I find leading the people of God away from the grace of God. From the God whose power is for salvation to all who believe and receive the merits of Christ's death by simple faith. I do confess to special harshness at times when I have penned my thoughts, and in attacking the individuals concerned I have not exhibited the gentle spirit of our Lord Jesus and have grieved His Holy Spirit. Yet the substance of what I have written, I shall not recant. If you can show me in the Scriptures how my teachings can be clearly proven wrong, I will most certainly recant all my views, build the largest bonfire Worms has ever seen, and tip all of my books into that blaze. But if you will not or cannot, then I will hold firm to my teachings."

Eck lost his temper in a blazing fury, taking off his red hat and, clutching it, smashing his fist into his other palm. His fellow priest rose from his chair, pointing an accusing finger at Martin. "You dare to put this council, your overseers, and this church to the test?" he roared.

Eck gripped the table tightly, his eyes blazing directly at Luther. "Your words are laughable, Luther. You hide behind the pages of the Bible when the pope and all the traditions of the church bear witness to what you should believe regarding it! It is to the church and to the Holy Father that you give your loyalty to hope for Christ's mercy. Who are you, a mere monk, to say God has revealed true grace to you in the pages of Scripture?"

Martin looked at Prince Frederick and saw he had closed his eyes in prayer. Turning back to Eck with renewed strength, Martin smiled and, turning his palms upward, replied with a joy that lit up his face! "Yes, I am a mere monk, but I trust a magnificent Savior! No pope, no council, no indulgence ... I place my trust in none of these! This alone is my hope and prayer, that I belong to Christ, who entered this world, lived, died, and rose from death for me! And He has ascended to Heaven and is constantly interceding with me to His Father who loves me with all gentleness and determination in spite of my sin! It is this Lord and Savior in Whom I find my everlasting hope, a King Whom I love because He first loved me! That above all things is the certain and constant confirmation given by Scripture, and unless I am convinced by Scripture itself or by plain, clear reason—because you must admit, popes and councils of the past have declared wrongfully before—I will *not* recant. I am bound by Scripture, God's Holy Word, and my conscience is held firmly captive by the Word of God."

Even Martin himself could not believe the change throughout the room. No one moved. No one spoke. There was no sound except for an occasional stifled cough or rustled paper. He went on.

"I cannot—and I will not—take back anything, for it is neither safe nor right to go against conscience. May God help and sustain me. Here I stand. I can do no other." He placed his hands on the table opposite Eck. "Amen."

The swarm of bodies that circled around him made more noise than the raging sea, and Martin winced at the pain in his ears. Frederick grasped his hand and pumped it wildly. "My young professor," he shouted, "you were magnificent. Now come, I have instructions for you."

"I don't know why," Martin replied, "for the church promised safe passage."

"Their promise," Frederick replied, "is why you need to come with me."

"Luther!" came a shout over the fray, and Martin turned to find himself face to face with his former friend.

"Martin," Eck said, whispering in his ear, "I tried. I surely tried. I will pray for you, but trust me, you are finished. It is finished."

Martin pulled Eck in front of him and looked him straight in the eye. "My Savior said those last three words on the Cross, good Eck. And because He did, I have enduring hope, no matter what you might believe otherwise."

MARTIN LUTHER emerged from his days in a monastery in Erfurt, Germany, as a teacher well-versed in Scripture but frightened of the holy judgment of God against sinners. Finding it impossible to earn God's favor by righteous living, Luther discovered the hope of God's grace in Romans 1:16-17 and found "the righteous shall live by faith." Convinced of the free grace of God in Jesus Christ, Luther both taught the Gospel clearly and spoke out against the abuses and falsehoods present in the Roman Catholic Church of his day. His Ninety-Five Theses, posted on October 31, 1517, spearheaded the Protestant Reformation, and his continued preaching earned him a rebuke from the pope himself. At Worms in 1521, Luther was called before the Diet for questioning. Johann Eck, a papal theologian (not to be confused with Luther's opponent of the same name at the Leipzig Debate of 1518), asked Luther if he was willing to renounce his errors and the works in which he had published them. Luther firmly stood his ground in defense of the Gospel of Jesus Christ, ensuring the Reformation would continue onward."

FACT FILES

Education, Literacy, and the Reformation

Today, maybe before you read this chapter, you briefly scanned an article on the Internet, intrigued by the headline. Or perhaps you were reading another book. Or you had to look over directions to assemble a bed from IKEA or to cook a meal with ingredients purchased from Tesco. In short, you had to make sense of words in front of you. You had to assess their meaning; you had to turn instruction into practical wisdom. In other words, you exhibited all the marks of an educated, literate person. If you can do that, then thank a Protestant Reformer.

Although we tend to take education for granted, it was not always that way. Even though champions of learning popped up in the Catholic Church in the Middle Ages (refer to the story of Theodulf of Orleans from the previous volume in this series), by the year 1500, education was largely the possession of the wealthy and the clergy. Education and literacy, when provided, focused almost exclusively on males. As the age of Luther, Calvin, and others gathered momentum, however, a hurricane of changes occurred that would transform education forever.

First, the Reformers were champions of *universal* education. No longer would schooling be a privilege of the upper-class males. Luther himself advocated that children of all economic levels, both male and female, must receive and pursue their God-given abilities under excellent teachers.[1] Reformers like John Calvin saw education as a key ingredient that could provide an avenue "for people to raise themselves ... and by

1. Keep in mind, this is what Luther and the Reformers advocated. Implementing a culture of this sort of change was not always successful in all places.

the diligent use of their knowledge and abilities." In addition, as the Reformation swept across Europe, so did the joint responsibility of church and home to reinforce classroom instruction. Churches were expected to provide funding for schools within their walls, and parents were to make certain their children attended class and completed their lessons at home.

Also, the Reformers enthusiastically pushed *integrated* education. For some time as an unspoken rule, teachers placed the study of religion at the top of a pyramid of subjects, with everything else arranged in a secondary role beneath religion. Reformers like Luther, Calvin, and others saw things differently. Education involved a particular view of the world as God's world. All of life, and therefore every subject, was important. And because God created His world, every subject was under His sovereignty and found its meaning in Him. Art became critically important. Mathematics underwent a resurgence of study. History and literature found renewed emphasis as disciplines that reflected the order and providence of God. And science in particular received great attention. Mark Thompson writes of Calvin believing that "science was a gift of God, created for the benefit of mankind. The real source of natural knowledge was the Holy Spirit. Whoever dealt with [science] acknowledged God, obeyed the call of God, and focused on God's creation. Thus, biology was also theology."

And the Reformers also pressed the matter of *transformative* education. Going to school was not merely a matter of working toward a diploma, going off to university, and securing a career with a sizable paycheck. The Reformation preached the truth that *education is not primarily for the good of the individual student, but to renew and restore God's world.* When students received quality instruction and achieved their results diligently and prayerfully, their lives would be shaped more and more to imitate Jesus Christ, with a hope to change their communities to how God wants them to be. Being educated with God's desires in mind, we can be part of doing God's will and—as the Heidelberg Catechism puts it—"everyone may carry out the duties of his office and calling as willingly and faithfully as the angels in heaven."

The spread of education also paralleled the spread of greater literacy. The Reformers expended great energy to make sure that people could read their own language. Thanks to the invention of Johannes Gutenberg's movable-type printing press in the fifteenth century, the publication of books became easier and cheaper. This included the printing of the Bible—in fact, one of the first books printed by Gutenberg was an edition of the Scriptures. Now, this was in the days when the Bible's sole translation was in Latin, which few ordinary people could understand when read to them, and even fewer could read it themselves! As the Reformers stressed that God's people should have God's Word in their own language, this passion brought on a flurry of activity. Martin Luther himself translated the entire Bible into German for his fellow citizens. William Tyndale—as we will see in another chapter—labored to produce the Scriptures in English so that the people of the British Isles could understand the Word of God. The Petri brothers, Olaus and Laurentius, received a commission from King Gustav Vasa to translate the Bible into the Swedish language. And Finland's Mikael Agricola, who studied under Luther in Wittenberg, returned to his homeland to produce a Finnish edition of the New Testament.

What these translations of the Bible did is nothing short of breathtaking. Luther's work produced not only a German Bible but also a unified German language.

In an age when different sections of the Holy Roman Empire would have various dialects of what passed for "German", Luther had to think about how to craft German vocabulary that a broad range of the population could grasp. The effect was that Luther ended up producing a recognizable, fresh, popular edition of German. For many years, Finnish was primarily a spoken language with little vocabulary written down. But through Mikael Agricola's dedication, that all changed. Taking the known sounds, Agricola produced an alphabet primer, a grammar book, and a booklet of catechism instruction of biblical truths for children. Finally, in 1548, after eleven years of hard work, Agricola's New Testament was printed, opening up an understanding of language and culture in what has since become the most literate nation in the world.

In a number of cases, the translation of the Bible brought about new written languages in the nations that received these Scriptures. For countries which had written languages and dialects, the new Bibles opened up greater understanding—not only of God's Word, but also of a world that people could enjoy in more vibrant color.

ULRICH ZWINGLI

April 1525, Zurich, Switzerland

The black-cloaked man clutched the wall as he turned around its corner into the main road through Zurich. His wife, knowing it was futile to remind her husband of the fresh rain on the street-stones, held her peace. He was otherwise occupied, and she knew why.

"To carry this burden alone, dear Ulrich," she had said before they left their modest house, "is not the command the Lord has given you. So why can't you tell me what this is about?"

Ulrich peered through the drizzling gloom toward the dwelling he knew well, situated less than seventy paces from the *Grossmünster*[1]. He could smell the aroma of roast meat and cabbage on the air. "This is not to burden you, dear Anna," he sighed. "And I am deeply sorry I have not offered you the travails of my heart. But to be truthful, I hardly know what awaits us tonight."

"I do not know why a meal at the Priels' would give you such anxiety," Anna replied, "nor why you desired our children to stay at our neighbors'. I should be at home with Regula and Gerold."

Stopping suddenly, nearly causing his wife to collide with him from behind, Ulrich quietly turned and slipped his right arm around Anna. "It is simply," he whispered, "that I want you to be here for two reasons. One is to

1. The Grossmünster ("great minster" or "great church") was the church that Ulrich Zwingli pastored in Zurich and was the initial centerpoint of the Reformation in Switzerland.

be my support. The other is so you might know the staggering road that is before me." He smiled painfully. "The wife of a pastor should know these things."

"I am glad you thoroughly enjoyed the meal," chuckled Konrad as he leaned back in his chair with the carved headpiece as his wife cleared the dishes from the table. His smile, though, disappeared with his next sentence. "But you, Ulrich, are an intelligent man. You know a mere supper is not the reason I asked you here tonight."

Ulrich reached underneath the linen cloth atop the table and grasped Anna's willing hand. "In two days' time," he announced, "I am to preach again at the Grossmünster, as anyone with ears within the walls of Zurich would know." He tensed the muscles in his upper back and continued. "Konrad, you are not telling me strange things. I think the reason we are here at this table is for you to make one more attempt to convince me not to preach."

"It is not the issue of you preaching, Ulrich," Konrad said gently, but with an edge in his voice noticed by both Ulrich and Anna. "It is both the substance of what you intend to say and the path upon which you will take this city. We have grown used to the images, candles, altars, priests' robes, and all manner of things, and you still are able to preach the Gospel as you will. One wonders why you cannot be content to let things remain as they are, and allow a more deliberate course for the reforms taking place in our city."

"A more deliberate course?" Anna blurted, amazed.

"Even you cannot deny the power of the Gospel that goes forth from the German lands, Ulrich, Anna," said Konrad. "Master Luther has given not a scrap of soil. He is unyielding to the Roman Church on the truth of the

Word of God and that all who are saved through Christ are granted His grace through faith, and faith alone. Yet even Luther has allowed worship to continue as structured by Rome."

"Provided," Ulrich interrupted, "that Scripture has not required anything to be changed."

"And tell me what is wrong with that?" Konrad questioned as his wife slipped out of the room to attend to their children.

"Simply this," Ulrich replied, leaning across the table. "If Scripture is God's Word, and if God's Word is completely true, and if we are to obey the Word of God, then we must ask how God has told us to worship Him ."

"Isn't that what we have been doing?" sputtered Konrad.

"It may appear that way, good Konrad," Ulrich replied, "but what you and others are doing—in opposition to the council of the city, mind you—is saying that whatever God has not forbidden is allowed in worship. I say we must submit ourselves completely to Almighty God. We must only worship Him in the way He has specifically directed. Has He told us to use candles, statues, pictures, crucifixes, and relics? Show me in Scripture where those things are and I will gladly let them stay!"

"But bless me," Konrad replied, cocking his head to his left, "we don't do that with the rest of our lives! When we make clothing, we don't wait upon God to direct us specifically from Scripture what materials are allowed. I could say the same about our dinner tonight! Or how I set out objects for sale in my shop? Why should we act one way for the rest of life and have the worship of God be so very different?"

"Simply because the worship of God *is* different, good Konrad," Ulrich sighed. "I am sorry that we so sorely disagree on this. I really am. But worshiping our Lord and Savior is the greatest thing we will do throughout our lives, and it will be the greatest joy we will enjoy in our life after death! If that is true, then certainly we must bend our will completely to the will of God revealed in His Word!"

Konrad spread his hands on the table, shaking his head slowly. "It is not just that, Ulrich," he muttered, "but that you seek so much for so many. You desire to bring everything this city does under the sway of the Lord Jesus and divine authority. It is much to deal with. It is much to risk. Does it not worry you that you could go too far in your break with the Roman Church and we could find ourselves to be targets of their military forces?"

"At least you are honest," sniffed Anna, "about your needless fears."

"Anna," said her husband, "he is allowed to speak his mind." Turning to Konrad, Ulrich said, "The break you speak of has been a long time in coming. It extends to the good we could be doing here in Zurich and the surrounding towns! The monasteries, for one, could be transformed for this purpose!"

"What do you mean?" asked Konrad.

"The ones who occupy these monasteries speak for days on end about helping the poor and blighted," Zwingli implored, his hands waggling in front of him as he gestured for effect, "but they live off the contributions of others while needy people languish. If we are to lift up the poor, the widows, the orphans, the blind and the lame, then we must eliminate the monasteries!"

"Get rid of the monks?" Konrad cried.

"Not the people themselves," Zwingli assured him, "but abolish the monasteries and use their structures to relieve those who are in deepest need. We have many sick in Zurich alone, so have the monasteries function as hospitals. Use their wealth to fund supplies for widows. Change the function of the churches to be houses for orphans! Our dear Jesus Christ said that whatever we do for the least of these, we do for Him! How can we not take Him at His word?"

Konrad's eyes darted left and right, his finger playing with a groove in the wooden top of the table. "I do not doubt your sincerity to have this city truly live out the Christian faith in all its fullness, Ulrich. But this is much to ask. You are wanting our people to run up a mountain when a walk on a gentle slope would be more agreeable! Cancelling the Mass. Ending processions of priests in worship. That was one thing. But now you are calling to go beyond that. You want to strip our churches of any beauty whatsoever. And other pastors who support your reforms have been practicing their own innovations in their churches. This is not order. This is chaos."

"I am not without compassion for your concerns, Konrad," said Zwingli. "And yes, we need order rather than disorder. But our Lord deserves to be worshiped in the manner He seeks to be adored. We will read the Scriptures. We will pray. We will sing. We will partake of the Lord's Supper as a meal of those nourished by grace. And we will proclaim the Word of God in a manner that the most intelligent of folk and the minds of babes can grasp its truth! What I can promise you is that I will rightly fear God above all the consequences I could face by being His servant."

The service on April 13th drew an overflowing crowd to the *Grossmünster.* As Ulrich looked up from his time of quiet prayer near the pulpit, he wondered how many people were here to support the new reforms, how many opposed him, and how many came out of pure curiosity. *O Sovereign Lord,* he prayed silently, *You know, and You will carry me through this hour.*

No choir stood behind him. There would be no processional up the aisle to begin the service. The simple pulpit, Ulrich had decided, would be enough, and he stepped behind it and looked upon the crowd murmuring below. After years of struggle, the day had come when the Latin Mass would be replaced by Zwingli's order of worship, written in German, so the people could participate fully. He looked at the people gathered in the *Grossmünster*, lifted his hands, and began to preach.

"The Apostle Paul declares in God's Word:

> *For I received from the Lord what I also delivered to you, that the Lord Jesus on the night when he was betrayed took bread, and when he had given thanks, he broke it, and said, 'This is my body, which is for you. Do this in remembrance of me.' In the same way also he took the cup, after supper, saying, 'This cup is the new covenant in my blood. Do this, as often as you drink it, in remembrance of me.' For as often as you eat this bread and drink the cup, you proclaim the Lord's death until he comes* (1 Corinthians 11:23-26).

Oh, people of God gathered here today, do our hearts not burn within us when we hear those glorious words? To know that we are holy yet fallen from grace, and still God wills that He should recover us to His embrace in the sacrifice of His Son, Jesus Christ! Christ, Who is Man and God, has purchased for us an endless redemption. His suffering on the Cross satisfies His Father's justice perfectly forever, and we in unshakeable faith must rely upon Him! If we could save ourselves by our works, it would be needless for Christ to die. But Christ is our sacrifice! We need no other to stand in our place! By His single offering, He has purchased our salvation, and He will make holy those whom He declares holy! Thanks be to God!"

The passion of the words from the mouth of the tall and sturdy man in the pulpit overwhelmed the people. Many nodded and patted their hearts in assurance; others wept openly. Zwingli spoke with authority and conviction as a true man of God! He concluded his sermon and extended his hands to his congregation.

"With solemn thanksgiving," he called, "let us pray to the Lord who redeemed His people."

The people bowed their heads as one, and Zwingli began to pray. "O Lord God Almighty, through your Holy Spirit you have made us into your united body in the unity of faith, and you have commanded this body to give you praise and thanks for your kindness and for the free gift of giving your only begotten Son, our Lord Jesus Christ, into death for our sin. We pray, grant that we do this faithfully so that we do not provoke the sincere truth to anger with any kind of hypocrisy and deceit. Grant also that we live so innocently and properly as your body, your servants, and your children that unbelievers also learn to know your name and honor. Lord, protect us so that your name and honor are never slandered because of our lives. Lord, everywhere and always increase our faith, that is, our trust in you, who lives and reigns, God eternally! Amen!"

The people uttered a powerful "Amen" in response, both shaken and emboldened by the power of hearing these words in their own language! Wasting no time, Zwingli announced, "In thanksgiving to our Savior God, let us recite a psalm of praise together."

Standing together, the congregation began on Zwingli's lead. Amazingly, no organ or instruments were used as in the singing of years past. Zwingli had declared them unnecessary, and given the volume of sound from the worshipers in the great church, Zwingli himself had made the right decision. The swell of the voices and passion of their chants filled the church with joy!

At the end of the singing, Zwingli and his assistants came to the floor below and brought some plain tables, with no jeweled chalices or sparkling bowls. They laid plain white cloths on the tables, and, placing wooden bowls and cups upon them, filled them with the bread and wine. Finally, surprising the people even more, Zwingli beckoned his assistants to join him—not facing the table, but going behind it and facing the people gathered in eager expectation. With a warm smile and hands uplifted, his voice practically sang out.

"To this table, our Lord Jesus calls all those who love Him, who have examined their hearts, who know their continual need of Him, that we might remember His death until He comes again."

The assembly, unsure the invitation literally meant to draw near, shuffled forward by ones and twos, but before long they began to press forward. Zwingli and his assistants distributed the bread and wine to those who came, blessing them, praying for them. Finally, Zwingli looked up and saw Konrad standing at the table, tears streaming down his cheeks. Zwingli smiled and held out a piece of bread.

"Christ has given Himself for you, Brother Konrad."

Konrad blinked and took the bread gratefully as Zwingli held out the cup to him. "Wooden bowls and cups," he whispered.

"Yes," Zwingli whispered back, "as I implied, quite ordinary, as they should be."

"Which is good, Pastor Ulrich," Konrad replied, his face beaming. "Ordinary vessels are good, for what matters is that we remember an extraordinary Savior!"

Sometimes called the "forgotten Reformer", **ULRICH ZWINGLI** was a true pioneer of the Protestant Reformation in Zurich, Switzerland. Navigating a path that differed from the Catholic establishment, Luther's views on worship, and radical reformers' more separatist ideas, Zwingli stressed distinctions that would shape the future of the Swiss Reformation. Valuing clear biblical preaching, the importance of educated ministers, transformation of worship into the language of the people and a simpler structure, and God's sovereignty in redemption, he served faithfully as a champion of spiritual reformation. Despite his untimely death in the battle of Kappel in 1531, Zwingli's solid trust in Christ alone for salvation and his commitment to the Bible lit a fire that showed the way to future church renewal.

PATRICK HAMILTON

January 1528, St. Andrews, Scotland

"Master Hamilton! Master Hamilton!" The cry was barely audible over the waves that crashed onto the Castle Sands. "Master Hamilton!" Callum called out again toward the lone figure, deep in thought, oblivious to the salt spray that flew around him. Picking up the fringe of his robe to make his way over the mushy sand, while mindful of the stones that pocked the beach's surface, Callum raced to his red-haired friend, nearly out of breath.

"Master Hamilton!" he said more sharply than he intended and seizing the man's arm. As if awakened from a deep sleep, Patrick Hamilton shook himself from his meditation, looking around to see where in fact he might be!

"Callum!" he exclaimed, looking over his friend's haggard appearance. "Why are you so out of breath?"

"And why are you here on the sands rather than preparing for your defense in the cathedral?" Callum asked, gasping for air, as a wave pounded upon the rocks nearby.

"Ah, yes, the disputation," Patrick nodded his head knowingly and craning his neck to look over the heights of the cliff toward the cathedral tower. His demeanor was serious, and he looked much older than his twenty-three years of age. "I merely came down here to breathe my Lord's fresh air once more and think upon His sufficient Word yet again. Surely that is no crime."

"It is not, Master Hamilton," Callum replied, "yet I would rather no one interpret your tardiness as impudence." He turned to see two others approaching. "Perhaps we can all convince you to come with us."

"Indeed, Master Hamilton," called Malcolm, approaching on his left. "The hour for your declaration has arrived, and I do believe the cathedral would provide a warmer environment for your sermon!"

"It would be better than this wind that cuts with the force of a thousand blades," quipped Callum.

"Then I shall come with you," Patrick allowed. "Even if I am headed into the dark shadow's valley, there the Lord will be with me."

"You seem to have given the twenty-third Psalm a great deal of thought," Malcolm smiled warmly.

"For it gives me all comfort," Patrick replied as they began the climb up the path near the castle, "to know my Shepherd's rod and staff protect me even as I go into the darkness just before me."

"Not to doubt the Savior's protection over you, good sir," Callum interjected, "but it seems to me that Lord Beaton has merely set a trap before you masquerading as an opportunity to preach."

"And although your relative the king is no friend of your convictions," added Malcolm, "it is notable that the clergy have encouraged him to go hunting up in the Highlands. So you are without any protection through your royal connections."

Patrick stumbled on a loose stone before gathering his footing. "And to that, friends, I say this: First, the King of Heaven grants me protection, not any earthly king. And any chance to preach the Scriptures is to be seized, for what others might intend for evil, God means for good."

"Even if it should lead to your death, Master Hamilton?" asked Callum.

And here Patrick looked quite thoughtful before a smile creased his face. "Everything leads to death, good Callum.

And one death can lead to life greater than a single grave." They turned at the top of the path as the cathedral rose before them to the left.

The glow of the candles lit up the normally dark interior of the cathedral as the assembly erupted in chatter over Patrick's arrival. The university students had occupied an entire section on the south side of the nave, and Patrick could see some of the Benedictine monks clustered in the north seats, Callum and Malcolm among the friendlier of that contingent. Nodding to them, Patrick strode resolutely to the altar at the east of the church, where he saw two gentlemen speaking in hushed tones, one dressed in cardinal red, the other in a black robe adorned with a white tippet.[1]

"Archbishop," Patrick spoke firmly and kindly. "Lord Abbot. Good morning to you both."

The red-clad James Beaton took a measured view of the youthful Patrick. "Master Hamilton," he said, scowling slightly but noticeably, "I am pleased and somewhat surprised you came. Welcome back to St. Andrews."

"Why indeed would you be surprised, Archbishop?" Patrick replied sternly. "Truth runs from no man, and your good nephew, my Lord Abbot was kind enough to see to my safe arrival."

"I hope you do not doubt our good intentions to have a proper disputation and allow you to preach your convictions publicly to those present," said the younger Beaton, David by name. "Indeed, what do you have to fear?"

"Nothing, Lord Abbot, as Christ Himself is with me having pledged His blood on my behalf."

"As long as we can hear you pledge yourself to the Holy Mother, your church, as well," Archbishop Beaton remanded.

1. A tippet is a long piece of cloth worn over the shoulders and draped down the front of a minister's body over a robe.

Patrick turned and fixed the archbishop with an icy stare. "The church, as any with common sense shall attest, did not give her life for my sake, Archbishop."

"Watch yourself, good Patrick," James Beaton warned coolly, "and show more gratitude for our security of safe conduct while you dwell here."

Patrick looked at the pulpit from which he would preach in mere moments. "For your nephew the Lord Abbot's arrangement for me to come, I am grateful, for more shall hear of the gospel of Christ that His enemies seek to suppress. But you know as well as I, Archbishop, that the same promise of safety was made to John Hus in Constance just over a century ago, and we know his prize was the burning stake."

He turned to climb into the pulpit. David Beaton drew to the side of his uncle the archbishop and took his arm. "Good uncle, have a care. His words are likely to exhilarate the masses today. And he is smelling a trap."

"He smells one because it is there, nephew," spat Archbishop Beaton as they shuffled to their seats.

"Master Hamilton," came the voice of Friar Campbell from the floor, "while it is admirable that you hold to your convictions with such ferocity, doesn't it give you some anxiety to know that your relative the king has denounced your views and labels the books of Luther as *cursed heresies*?"

"Professor," Patrick called out from the pulpit, "if someone offered you the clearest, purest water to quench your deepest thirst, would you restrain yourself if all the kings of earth called it evil to drink?"

"You are not here to speak in riddles, Hamilton!" barked the Archbishop. "Answer the question directly!"

"Then it is to the university or the church to ask me a question of substance regarding my beliefs," Patrick sighed, "and not these pricking contentions of possible anxiety. The truth of the Gospel fears no human threat."

The crowd murmured in approval, particularly the university students. Campbell waved for them to be quiet and turned on the young preacher. "Then let our disputant give his reasons why he hates the commandments that our Lord gave to the prophet Moses, the people of Israel, and to our dear church which receives Christ's children within its hands."

Patrick gripped the sides of the pulpit tightly. He thought, *So, they are determined to throw any manure at all upon the sweetest of the truth of Christ? So be it.*

"You well know that no one can rightly call himself a Christian if he bears such hatred of the law of God, not merely that of the Ten Commandments but also of the two great commandments of which Christ Himself reminds us: To love God with all one's heart, mind, soul, and strength and to love your neighbor as oneself. I bear no hatred of God's instruction, good professor and all assembled here today, for He has given us His law for our good. I simply mean to declare clearly the *limitation* of what God's law can do."

"The instruction which we are to keep?" Archbishop Beaton snarled. "You dare to turn us away from that?"

"I say it is impossible to keep the moral law of God. You have fashioned a path for people to walk so they might sense their own righteousness, O churchmen! But no!—God gave us His law and commandments for the express purpose of displaying how impossible it is to keep it as we should, which is absolute perfection. God's law shows us we are hopelessly evil and helplessly separated from Him. All the Law can do is batter and command. It cannot make us worthy or noble or good! That is the task of the glorious Gospel of Christ!"

"How dare you say the Law is powerless!" Campbell hissed as the students roared with approval for Patrick's boldness.

Patrick looked down and saw both Callum and Malcolm smiling amidst the monks before turning his attention to Campbell. "Not so! God's commands have power in that they show us our deepest need, as a pane of glass might show me the dirtiness of my face. Then I know I must clean it! But can the glass purify the filth that clings to my cheeks, my forehead, and my mouth? No! I need something else for that which the glass cannot provide!"

"But the church has declared that you are duty bound to partake in such goodness as the Sacraments, of good works and charity, to make the good deposit by which grace might be dispensed to you!" the archbishop roared.

"You have the chair that gives you the right to interject, Your Grace!" Patrick thundered back with power that shook the beams of the cathedral. "It does not mean what you speak is true!"

"How dare you!" Campbell gasped.

"Do any here truly imagine that the pages of Holy Scripture show us any hope that we can justify ourselves, that by our actions we can gain good footing before our Lord God?" Patrick asked stridently. "The Law says to us, 'Pay up your debt to God!', but the Gospel assures us 'Christ has paid that debt!' The Law identifies us as desperate and miserable sinners, but the Gospel assures us that in Christ, our sins are forgiven! The Law tells us, 'Because of your sin, you shall surely die!' The Gospel comforts us and says, 'Because of Christ, you are saved!' The Law declares, 'Make amends for your waywardness!', while the Gospel shouts, 'No! For Christ has already made amends for you!' The Law brings the thunder of God's wrath, but the Gospel offers the gentle refreshment that Christ's blood turns aside the Father's wrath! The Law asks, 'Where is your righteousness?', while the Gospel proclaims, 'I find it in Christ!' The Law says, 'You deserve the fire of hell!', but the Gospel reminds us that Jesus delivered us from hell by enduring it on the glorious Cross!'"

"Christ, Christ, Christ!" bellowed the archbishop. "All you speak of is Christ on end with no love for the church herself!"

"Simply because, Your Grace," Patrick shouted, lunging forward with such force that he nearly toppled from the pulpit to the floor below, "Christ is our Savior who died for us, for our sins as the perfect offering once for all, bearing our sins on His back, redeeming us and washing us white as snow in the reddest of holy blood! He alone is our righteousness, our wisdom, our sanctification, our redemption, our satisfaction, our goodness, and our only hope! Only by this do we have life, in trusting that the Father has forgiven us for Christ's sake!"

"What in God's name do you expect the church to do, then?" Beaton snapped. "Are you willing to blaspheme God and His church by saying we have nothing we must do to partake of the salvation the church bears?"

"Nothing?" Patrick retorted, his arms spread wide as the assembly shouted their encouragement. "Nothing? Of course, we have a response, but this is where you and I differ, where the enemies of God and the Gospel collide! Do you really propose to act as the rich young ruler before Christ Himself, asking 'What good thing must I do for eternal life'? We *believe* the Gospel, good people. Listen and mark it well! Receive and rest upon the promise of Christ's perfect sacrifice! Take Jesus at His word and let your lives show you act upon those precious promises of the Gospel! What is a savior but the one who rescues? Do you mean, Archbishop, that you believe you can save yourself by your actions and charity? Are you putting yourself in the place of Christ? And if that be the case, then aren't *you* the one who commits blasphemy?"

The cathedral erupted in a massive tumult—churchmen, monks, students, and professors speaking and yelling in response to Patrick's courageous and forceful display. The gesturing and finger-pointing continued long after Patrick descended from the pulpit and walked toward the altar, where some quizzical university students had gathered to ply him with earnest questions.

Scowling at the base of the pulpit, James Beaton gripped his archbishop's crook so tightly his knuckles turned ghostly white. Seeing the flashes of fire in his uncle's eyes, the Lord Abbot touched his arm and whispered in his ear, "Good sir, you knew the risks in having Hamilton come here for a disputation. We cannot destroy him, and yet we cannot allow his infection to rage through our nation."

"What are we to do?" the archbishop hacked once he found his voice. "He came here by our invitation, and each step he takes is like a stroke of the pen signing his own death warrant." Beaton paused, rubbing his forehead, oddly sweaty in the frigid cathedral. "And yet, I am afraid that if we execute him, we will only fan the flames of his teaching throughout the whole of Scotland."

PATRICK HAMILTON's vibrant faith found courage and depth when he studied in Europe at Paris and Wittenberg, where he became convinced of the teachings of Martin Luther. Upon returning to Scotland, he spent the better part of a month in St. Andrews preaching and disputing on behalf of the Gospel of Christ. In the end, Archbishop James Beaton had Patrick arrested at the cathedral on the morning of February 29, 1528. The twenty-three-year-old reformer endured a sham trial and baseless accusations overseen by Friar Campbell before being taken to St. Salvador's Chapel at the university. Condemned to death, he was burned at the stake for six hours before finally uttering "Lord Jesus, receive my spirit" as his heart beat for the final time. Confirming the deepest fears of Archbishop James Beaton, his courage and teaching spread throughout the nation and launched the Scottish Reformation.

FACT FILES

The Reformation and Worship

We have mentioned how the Protestant Reformation brought about a shift in the way the church proclaimed salvation, how one is *made right* with God so one might live for God. As the medieval church had reversed those concepts, the Reformation put them together in their biblical order. The Reformers' stress upon the principles of Scripture alone, Christ alone, faith alone, grace alone, and for God's glory alone rooted the believer's life in the joy of being captured by the indescribable and undeserved mercy of Jesus Christ.

But this shift in doctrine led to a shift in practice as a spiritual community of faith. Re-discovering grace led the Reformers to re-discover how that was expressed in worship. And this is only natural. Our worship of God is an outgrowth of what we believe about God, and it should cause us to rejoice in Almighty God.

For years throughout the Middle Ages, the Roman Catholic Church had developed a system of worship known as the Mass (from the Latin phrase, "*Ite, missa est*", meaning "Go, it [the congregation] is dismissed"). The Mass was the principal weekly worship service for Catholics in Europe, a ritual that offered some beginning prayers, Scripture readings, a short sermon or homily, followed by a saying of a creed, prayers over the offerings, and finally the Eucharist—or Holy Communion—before dismissal.

While the order of the Mass evolved into this sequence over the Middle Ages, what the Reformers were facing during their time was a host of matters they desired to change. For one, the Mass was spoken, chanted, or sung in Latin. While the priests leading the service could have a working knowledge of Latin (and, by the way, some didn't!), it would be difficult to find an ordinary churchgoing Catholic who did. A number of the people in any medieval church didn't even know how to read or write their own language, let alone Latin. The church leadership, however, doggedly maintained the use of Latin since Jerome had translated the Bible into Latin, which the Catholic Church upheld as its official version. Also, the priests spoke and chanted much of the service themselves, facing the altar away from the congregation, so they could address God. The people were not left with much to do other than follow along—which the priests believed would force them to pray devotedly on their own since they couldn't understand any of the service. Yes, the priests believed that *not knowing what was going on* could benefit the people spiritually. And when the time came for the Eucharist, on the rare time the people could come forward to receive at the Communion altar, they would be given only bread. As the medieval church believed the bread and wine were turned into the body and blood of Jesus, priests held back from giving people the cup of wine, for fear they would spill the "blood".

So, worship in the late Middle Ages was a non-understandable experience in which most of the people could not participate fully. The church was becoming two classes of individuals: the clergy who would be active and the laity who were not. It was when the Reformation came along that not only did theology change, but the philosophy of worship shifted with the force of a hurricane. While there were some distinctions and differences amongst the Protestant leaders regarding worship, there were some profound similarities that united them.

Perhaps the most radical shift in worship in the Protestant Reformation was the full participation of the congregation in the service of praise and communion. One of the teachings of the Reformers was the "priesthood of all believers", taken from I Peter 2:5, in which followers of Jesus are called a *royal priesthood.* Placing clergy and laity on the same level of importance in the eyes of God meant that both had a necessary role in worship. The people's energy wasn't merely hoped for; it was expected. And while this was evident in many ways, four particular areas come to mind.

First, the Reformers firmly believed that worship should be conducted in the vernacular, the language of the people where they lived. This meant if a congregation worshiped in Paris, they should worship in French! In York, it would be in English! In Zurich or Wittenberg, German. In Helsinki, Finnish. And in restoring worship into the local language, the Reformers did not view themselves as doing anything radical, but were rather restoring worship to the manner of the ancient church. They would point to events like Pentecost, where the Holy Spirit empowered the apostles to speak in languages they did not know *so that the many people gathered in Jerusalem from all over the Roman Empire could hear the message of Jesus intelligibly in their own language.* Therefore, the vernacular in worship had biblical foundations.

The people's language was the first step, but to assist them even more, the Reformers knew an understandable *structure* was needed, so many of them wrote **liturgies** to be used in worship. "Liturgy" may be an unfamiliar word for some of us; for others, we may think of "liturgical churches" where there are a lot of spoken parts or responsive readings involving the congregation. In truth, *liturgy* comes from the Greek language and means "public labor" or "the work of the people". Therefore, a written or understood liturgy would give all worshipers a sense of order and structure so they could do the "work" of worship together. For churches in Strasbourg, Martin Bucer produced a liturgy for Sunday worship. Zwingli had done likewise in Zurich, Luther in Germany, and Calvin in Geneva. Thomas Cranmer produced an entire book of worship services, the Book of Common Prayer, to be used by English Christians! Yes, there were some differences among them. The placement, subject, and length of the prayers would vary, as would the placement of the sermon, how the congregation would approach Communion, and what type of singing there would be[1], but the common denominator was that all the people were involved.

Another piece of evidence that showed congregational participation was the sermon. I do not mean that anyone could preach; ordained ministers were the ones expected to deliver sermons. But now the Scriptures were proclaimed in the language of the people, so everyone who was worshiping could hear the Bible explained in a way they could understand. The Reformers took seriously Jesus' command to the apostle Peter, "Feed my sheep." (John 21:15-17) If God's people are His lambs, then those who preach must give them spiritual food they could properly digest![2] This objective was twinned with another principle of preaching: the minister must present Law and Gospel every time he preached, so that the people could clearly understand God's demands, our sin and failure to meet God's demands, and the good news of Christ's redemption that provides the hope we need. No longer was the sermon an exercise in priestly knowledge; it was to pour fresh hope and courage into followers of Jesus so they could boldly worship Him and expectantly participate in Communion.

Speaking of the sacraments—baptism and the Lord's Supper—they were elements which became more a part of

1. For example, Luther wrote many hymns himself, Calvin preferred the singing of Psalms, and Zwingli desired no musical accompaniment at all!

2. This also made some impact on the layout of some Reformed churches. Calvin, for example, had the pulpit set above, so it would be elevated over the Communion table. This was part of his conviction to demonstrate the sacraments receive their power from the Word of God, not the other way around.

congregational life. This is especially so with the sacrament of Communion. Participation went beyond the clergy and the congregation regularly partook of the Supper. Luther directed his hearers to the words of Jesus during the Last Supper: "Take, eat, this is my body which is given *for you*. Take and drink of it, *all of you*, this is the cup of the new and eternal testament in my blood, which is poured out for you and for many for the forgiveness of sins." Surely since Jesus intended His followers then to participate in His meal, He intended His followers at any time, to do so, as well? Calvin spoke of the necessity of the sacraments for God's people calling them symbols "by which the Lord seals in our consciences the promises of His good will toward us, to sustain the weakness of our faith." And Thomas Cranmer noted that Christians should receive Christ's gifts in full: "The Cup of the Lord is not to be denied to the Lay-people: for both the parts of the Lord's Sacrament, by Christ's ordinance and commandment, ought to be ministered to all Christian men alike."

Yes, there was variety amongst the Reformers on the issue of worship. Some were more formal than others; some were stricter on what could and could not be in a worship service. But virtually all of them were united on that most biblical and revolutionary of truths: worship was truly the work of the people for the glory of God."

MARGUERITE DE NAVARRE

April 5, 1531, Nerac, France

"My queen," came the breathless voice of Isabelle as she scampered down the hallway from the royal apartment, "are you certain it is wise? You have said yourself how dangerous it is, so why should you desire to carry out this wish?"

Marguerite, the Queen of Navarre, stopped, her toes curling into the lavish rug of the hallway, as if the exercise could release her own tension. Squaring her shoulders and slowly turning to her lady's maid, she placed her hands together. "There is no need to be so anxious, Isabelle. In fact, it need not happen here in the apartments." She paused, looking very thoughtful. "Will you go to the chapel at any time today?"

"I can be there on angel's wings in a moment's notice for you, my lady," Isabelle offered willingly.

"Then do this: Go and see the priest there. Tell him the time has come for us to be together as the Psalmist directs."

"What do you mean by that?" Isabelle replied, her face scrunched in confusion.

"I was thinking of how King David wrote, 'If I make my bed in the grave, you are there.' To be frank, Isabelle, today we must go to the grave to meet our Savior."

"The grave?"

"Tell the priest I said there is no place so low that the presence of God is not there. He will understand, I am sure. Then come back to me and we will gather there at half past the next hour."

The candles flickered, casting dancing shadows upon the walls of the cellar. The labyrinthian walk had taken longer than Marguerite expected, and Isabelle and the rest of the queen's court who knew of the plan followed her into the cool, damp room. Though another room now housed the casks of the palace wine, one could see the remnants of the shelving from when this room stored the libations that were a staple of dinners in the great hall.

"Father Roussel," the queen cheerfully spoke as she approached the priest, "I am glad that you understood exactly what I intended."

"It is good we both have minds that understand nuance, and that is encouraging." He lit the candles on the long table that would serve as a makeshift altar before continuing. "Speaking of encouragement, I have word that my friend and your correspondent Jacques Lefèvre intends to come here soon, if you will host him."

"Jacques Lefèvre! Here! But of course, he must," Marguerite exclaimed. "I would be so willing to give him quarters here in Nerac, as I know you must be thrilled at the idea."

"He provided me spiritual light when I possessed only darkness," said Father Roussel. "Of course, he should be welcome, if that be your desire, of course, Your Majesty."

The room had filled to at least thirty people, and a servant who brought up the rear closed the door. Drawing near to the priest, Marguerite entreated, "Father, after the service of Communion is ended, permit me to speak a few words. I know it is unusual, but I do insist."

"It is a Wednesday in Lent as we approach the weekend of our Lord's death and resurrection, and we are in a cellar," the priest smiled broadly. "I am prepared to overlook unconventional actions, Your Majesty."

The service was completed in forty minutes time, pleasing Marguerite greatly as she knew there would be plenty of time for her to address their small assembly before her husband the king returned from his hunt. She had prayed fervently through most of the service as the words of the liturgy washed over her. She listened intently to the Scripture readings. When the small group chanted "Alleluia" or joined in the Creed, she responded with them. And she gave her entire attention to the earnest—if unpolished—sermon given by Father Roussel. All the worshipers went forward to receive the bread and wine, Marguerite waiting until the last out of kindness and respect for her entire court. She strode forward, bowing near the altar as Father Roussel stood before her and placed the bread in front of her lips. Surprising him and herself, she lifted her hands and took the bread from him.

"If you please," she said in a hushed tone, "I wish to hold it for a moment before I partake."

She pressed the crust of bread, not to her lips, but to her nose. Sniffing in deeply, she prayed with all her heart. "You are truly good to me, Lord Jesus. For all the trials I endure, You have endured even more suffering in your all-sufficient sacrifice. Your body, your arms stretched out on the hard wood of the Cross, given for me. May I remember Your grace for me until my final breath, whenever it may come."

The priest turned to the altar when Marguerite finally placed the morsel in her mouth, but the queen whispered, "Father Roussel, the cup."

The priest was taken aback. "Your Majesty, it is the blood of our Lord. Shouldn't the bread be sufficient?"

"Shouldn't you be less superstitious of a queen spilling the cup of Christ? I desire to drink of it, Father." Placing her hands with his on the simple pewter chalice, she raised it to her lips, murmured a prayer, and sipped.

"The cup of salvation, Your Majesty," Roussel said. "May it keep you in everlasting life."

Marguerite returned to her seat for the concluding prayers and responses. When the priest blessed the small congregation, he asked for silence. After several moments, he then looked over at the queen, nodded, and moved to the side to grant her space.

Marguerite looked at her fellow gatherers. So much of what they did had to be in secret. She thought of the hopeful advances they had made for the free worship of the Protestant faithful throughout France. And those hopes had drawn many to their location in Nerac, but mainly because of the now-increasing persecution. She thought of her brother's initial kindness now soured, his tolerance since turned to coldness. All her troubles she had endured, the loss of a child to death, and now what she was about to share with her friends gathered there, the loss of another. Everywhere she lived, she fought for those who desired to worship and trust Christ in the freedom of His grace and love. Everywhere she lived, hardship followed. And now she had to speak of more.

"My fellow pilgrims," she began—always with the tender address of *pilgrims*, never *subjects*, "I thank you for joining me today in the depths of this palace. It is true that we risk much in our reception of our Savior's grace, in the hearing of the very pure Word of God and feasting at His table. But there would be much more to risk if we disdained such wondrous worship.

"But I do not wish that you be unaware of the troubles that may lie ahead. Of course, I desire you to walk that road with me, but may it be by free choice, not because I am your queen who presses you with a rod of iron. Kings may threaten in such ways, but I never will. I have made no secret of my allegiance to the reforming truths from Germany and Switzerland, and some of my former ladies now resident in England tell me that the light of Christ's grace is breaking into the darkness there. Such actions of the Holy Spirit of God give me great hope."

Isabelle stood meekly and asked, "I do not mean to speak out of turn, my lady, but of what troubles do you speak?"

"I simply mean that the persecution that is spreading across France as we speak will only come to us, as well," said Marguerite firmly. "In truth, it has already begun. Although it is good to come to our Savior's table here away from spying eyes, it is not the first time it has happened. Many of you were here with us in this very space a few years ago. Coming here, we risk much again."

Father Roussel, attempting to calm the tense atmosphere, spoke up. "My queen, everything we do takes a chance, but why do you use the word 'again'?"

"Because of something I have kept private from all of you. Do you recall that day we met here before?"

The assembly nodded their assent.

"Then you remember that when Henri, my husband and Navarre's king, returned from his hunt that day, word had somehow reached him about 'the fastings in the cellar', as he termed them, and he stormed to my room."

"We never heard him," Isabelle urged.

"You had told us to leave and go to the other end of the palace, O queen," Roussel recalled.

"I did, but I never told you why," Marguerite choked out the words, remembering the savage conflict as if it were only the day before. "I asked you to leave me alone with my servants—none of whom are here, you will notice—and Henri stormed into my bedchamber, red-faced and as destructive as a snowstorm in the Pyrennes. He berated me for my 'insufficient religion', as he called it. He screamed at me, calling me an unsubmissive cow, and then, to my terror, he struck me in the face. First on the left, and then backhanding me on my right cheek, he cried, "Madame, you know too much! Would that God strike you down before you pretend to know His ways!"

"That was when you had the bruises on your face," Isabelle remembered. "When I asked you what happened, you said, 'It is nothing, let it pass.'"

"That was not untrue, dear Isabelle," the queen answered. "It was truly no great thing. And my brother dealt with it at that time."

"Was that when King Francis arrived with his army?" asked a page several feet behind Isabelle. "Did he threaten King Henri over his treatment of you?"

"My brother and I might not agree on religion," Marguerite allowed, "but he was not going to allow another man to strike me. He threatened war upon Navarre unless Henri begged me in tears for my forgiveness, which I granted him. And I must say Henri has shown sincerity after that. He does allow us to hold these services and for the teachings on Scripture from men like Luther and Zwingli to have a place here. He even reads such works himself. I must say he has kept his side of the agreement."

"Then why do you speak of trouble, if your husband will grant such leniency?" asked Isabelle.

"Because the tolerance that my brother, Francis, ruler of all France, had extended in years past has disappeared like the rain during the days of Elijah the prophet," the queen replied. "He traveled recently to Spain and came under the spell of the Archbishop of Madrid, returning a different man. He has banned any Protestant books from his jurisdiction and is turning a blind eye to the persecution of many of Christ's faithful followers, simply because they are not Catholic."

"You say this, Your Majesty," Roussel cautioned, "even though you remain with Rome."

"I do so," Marguerite shot back, eyes flashing, "to do my part to transform my church from a citadel of increasing corruption and wearying spirituality to one in which the clear rivers of God's grace wash over the souls of those who confess their need of Him! And that has cost me dearly. It has cost me peace with my brother. It has cost me sleep at night. And it has cost me my daughter!"

"But Jeanne has not been here in six months!" Isabelle cried. "Wasn't she going to Paris, to the king's court, during Advent and Epiphany?"

"All of which was over two months ago, Isabelle," Marguerite shuddered, collapsing to the floor, tears blotting her cheeks, "during which time Francis sent word that—in his words—I had no need of my daughter Jeanne if I was intending to raise her as a Protestant! So, he has taken her away to bring her up as a French princess, under the guise of Roman priests, away from me!"

So raw was the memory that it was several minutes before Marguerite stopped crying. When she ceased her tears, she looked up, and everyone in the room had drawn close in a semicircle around her.

"Dear friends, my pilgrims, thank you," she sniffed. "I just always remember that they can take my daughter, but they can never take away from me the Christ who has atoned for my sin by His most precious blood!"

"It is still difficult, Your Majesty," said Isabelle, resting a comforting hand on the queen's arm.

"It is," agreed the queen as she struggled to her feet, helped by two pages, "and that is what has led me to perhaps be of comfort to all of you if we enter dark times. I have spent some time composing a poem of my own, remembering my own sin and dwelling upon the lavish love of God. I wish to share it with you now." She signaled to another lady's maid, who passed a parchment to the queen. "May I?"

"Of course, we will gladly listen," said Father Roussel.

"Is it the sort that the church will condemn?" asked the same male page who had spoken earlier.

"I am sure that there will be the occasional priest or monk who declares I should be sewn up in a sack and thrown into the Seine," Marguerite mused, "but as the apostle Paul comforts us, if God is for us, who can stand against us?"

The little circle around the queen sat, hushed and waiting for her words to spill over them. How long they remained there they could not say. It was a time of wondrous joy, for Marguerite of Navarre was bringing comfort and hope through the grace they knew was a gift of Christ alone.

"Such a deep abyss," she began, "is sufficient to punish my sins, so great in number that they cannot be counted. Such a great sinner am I."

And yet, the gathering knew that was not the end of the story, for as Marguerite read on, there was grace.

"And what is more, I claim that none other than Jesus Christ is my defender. Our Advocate before God offers us virtues of such worth, that my debt is more than paid."

Amen, whispered her friends around her. *Amen.*
There was grace. There would always be grace.

MARGUERITE DE NAVARRE, (1492-1549) queen of the region of Navarre in France, promoted the ideas of Reformation in the French kingdom even though she risked much doing so. Her younger brother Francis became King of France and personally defended his sister's desire for reform even though he remained a committed Catholic. Marguerite welcomed many French reformers to her palace at Nerac, including Jacques Lefèvre, William Farel, and John Calvin. Her relationship with Anne Boleyn—King Henry VIII of England's second wife—assisted in the English Reformation, while her daughter Jeanne d'Albrecht managed to hold firm to the Protestant faith.

Though Marguerite remained a Catholic all her life, her passion for Reformation teaching and her defense of its biblical faithfulness led her to try to reform the Catholic Church to the best of her ability. As a result, the French Reformed Church that grew in her nation owed her a debt of thanks for her patience and protection.

WILLIAM TYNDALE

April 1535; Antwerp, Habsburg Netherlands

The creak from the floorboards resounded through the house, and Thomas Poyntz grimaced, fearing less about any structural damage than he did about disrupting the work of his guest. Taking the lit candle with him, Poyntz edged the door to the back room open and peeked in, expecting to see the translator bent over his labors at the wooden desk. Surprisingly, he found his guest seated in a chair, back turned toward the desk and the sheaves of paper piled upon it. Rather than the usual air of urgency about the room, Poyntz discerned an atmosphere of contentedness and joy. He placed the candlestand down on a nearby table and grinned broadly.

"My good Tyndale, it is as unexpected as it is glorious to see you in this state," Poyntz beamed. "To what do we owe this sudden change of disposition?"

William Tyndale leaned forward, rubbed his hands as if releasing the weariness from them, and returned Poyntz's smile. "The good news of every writer, my good Thomas," he replied. "I have two reports of good news, in fact. Would you like to hear them?"

"Would I like to hear them?" Poyntz scoffed in a playful manner. "You are my esteemed boarder and you wonder if I wish to know of how the providence of the Lord has fallen upon you anew? Of course, I wish to know the news!" He sat in a chair across the room from Tyndale. "By all means, proceed!"

Tyndale pulled his cloak around him, shivering slightly. "The first has to do with my revision of the New

Testament. I have received word that the initial copies have made their way throughout England! The arrangements to ship them across the Channel were made quickly and I have already received word from friends at Oxford that many of our brothers are expressing immense joy for the privilege of so many receiving the Word of God in their own tongue!"

"This is indeed good news, Master William!" exclaimed Poyntz. "However, it befuddles me why you were able to ship them so successfully."

"Smuggled, of course," Tyndale replied, unable to keep the childlike smile from dancing on his lips. "Much like last time, I suppose. I was told it was likely a ship filled with crops for trade and my allies negotiated the placement of the copies under a massive volume of barley."

"And that worked?"

"The presence of God's Word in English throughout the countryside of our native land bears witness that it did."

"I am glad, Master William," said Poyntz, "although I confess to being somewhat surprised that port agents in Sandwich, New Romney, and other places would not have been wary of smuggling."

"To that," Tyndale replied, "I believe we must thank God in His mysterious provision. A poor harvest in parts of southern England brought on the need for more barley exported from here, as you recall. So, there were plenty of crops to hide my publications. And with that much barley, and the need to have it properly and quickly transported to those in need, many port agents would not want to take the time and labor to check for an unlawful shipment!"

"There is a message for us, I am sure," Poyntz mused, "in that event for how God's ways are greater than ours."

"And for how we approach each day under God's guidance," Tyndale replied. "As with the port agents, we often only see what is visible in any moment, and we assume that is all that is. But we fail to see God's true provision—like those many copies—which lie beneath the surface of what we see. So much of His work is hidden. We need to pray for eyes to see how near He is to us!"

Poyntz sat quietly for a few moments, drinking in the wisdom of his guest. *He has done so much for God's kingdom here in this little room,* he thought. *And William continues to see God's great work.* Rousing himself, he said, "And the second report of good news?"

Tyndale nodded before drawing his cloak more tightly around him. "Yes, I'd like to share that with you as well, but could we do so outside?"

"In the garden?"

"I was thinking a walk might be in order," Tyndale replied, rising from his chair.

"I really am quite unsettled by your desire to go about in public like this," Poyntz muttered to Tyndale as they strode through the streets of Antwerp. "You know that you are still a wanted man in England, and King Henry could very well have his spies about!"

"And we also have friends who have sharp ears and clear eyes, standing guard for our protection," retorted Tyndale. "So, I think you can calm your nerves and assume you will be paying me my stipend for some time to come."

"I wouldn't be so confident," grumbled Poyntz.

"We could always walk through the alleys."

"William, you know as well as I do that Antwerp's alleys aren't wide enough for two men to walk side by side. Our choices are either out here in front of God and the whole city, or my back garden."

"The alleys may not be wide enough," Tyndale groaned, "but they are safe enough."

"Regardless," said Poyntz impatiently, "what was your second report of good news?"

"Ah, that!" Tyndale responded, rubbing his hands gleefully. "I just finished another book!"

"I am glad my stipend is well used," Poyntz rejoined with a smile. "You certainly are earning every meal at my table."

"Each of them most delicious," said Tyndale.

"For that, you can thank my wife," Poyntz agreed, "and the fact that your esteemed host is a ranking member of the Worshipful Company of Grocers. But we are digressing. Your new book?"

"Yes, I have completed a work that I wish to call *A Pathway Into the Holy Scriptures*."

"A pathway? That's a rather intriguing title. What is this pathway for?"

"Yes, I thought about that. Some might think I mean a path to interpret and understand the Bible, and there is some truth to that perspective. But I mean to show the key to what Scripture truly shows us: the righteousness we require before God that we only find in our Lord Jesus Christ."

"That could fill several books, my good William."

"Indeed. I wish for this to be a guide so that people can understand our hope clearly. Christ alone—not our confessions nor any good works—is the source of our redemption. Any good that we do reveals Jesus' righteousness already applied to us. Therefore, all praise and glory be given to Christ alone."

"Soundly Scriptural," Poyntz added, "although you realize the Roman Church will see this as a further defiance?"

"They should," Tyndale said as they moved to avoid a horse-drawn cart headed past them and going in the direction of the River Scheldt. "After all, most of my revisions in my New Testament translation already demonstrate the great differences between the teaching of the Bible and the teaching of the pope."

"Master Tyndale!" called a voice from behind. Both Tyndale and Poyntz looked back to find a dapper, smiling figure approaching them on the walkway.

"Harry Phillips!" exclaimed Tyndale. "How good to see you!"

"Indeed," Thomas Poyntz demurred with considerably less enthusiasm. "You are a significant distance from your lodgings."

"For that, I must thank my host," said Phillips, brandishing several gold coins, "who has sent me to buy food for dinner tonight. In fact, we would love to have you for a meal some time, Master Tyndale!"

"Surely, a merchant like Stephen Pym is capable of extending the invitation himself as the master of his own house," offered the suspicious Poyntz.

Waving him off, Tyndale smiled graciously. "I accept. Let me know a good evening for such a meal ."

Bowing low, Phillips turned and bounded away. "I would beware of people like Harry Phillips, sir," said Poyntz. "We know so little about him."

"My friend," Tyndale replied in a demanding tone, "Harry has arrived in Antwerp in dire situations. He is a rather poor man, with few means. And yet he is one of the most faithful worshipers of Christ, and he brings such passion to our studies of Luther's works!"

"All I did was advise caution, sire. Our knowledge of him is minimal."

"What we do know is encouraging," Tyndale reminded him. "Now what were we discussing before Harry stopped us? My revisions of my New Testament translation, was it not?"

"Yes. And as a matter of curiosity," Poyntz asked, "how many revisions?"

"Over four thousand by my counting."

"Four thousand!"

"Yes," said Tyndale, "and also I am sure Rome was not happy with my keeping words from my original volume. Calling ministers 'elders' instead of 'priests' challenged them greatly. Re-naming the Greek word *ekklesia* as 'congregation' rather than 'church' upset many, especially the Bishop of London. He hated that I was proclaiming a true church was a group of true believers, not an institution. And to imply that ministers and ordinary believers alike were part of the same congregation made Bishop Stokesley think I meant we all function together in ministering the gospel of Christ."

"And weren't you doing just that?"

"I plead guilty," Tyndale said wearily. "It does concern me that so much of my life has been weighed down by hardship and controversy. But if salvation is by faith in Christ alone, then that transforms how we see the church. I can't hold back from that any more than I can refrain from putting God's Word into the language of ordinary people!"

"If there is one passion that stirs you more than anything," Poyntz said, "it is that. And it has burned within you for some time."

"Yes, it has. For years. And all because of a time when God sought to move me from where I was comfortable to where He desired me to be. And I do not speak of when I came to Antwerp."

Poyntz said nothing, content to let Tyndale continue his story.

"I was at Cambridge some fifteen years ago," Tyndale began, "and I was caught in the swirl of much excitement. A number of the works of Martin Luther had come to Cambridge, and the resulting discussion amongst the students created considerable excitement. Many of us searched the Scriptures with renewed zeal and exuberance, we debated Luther's teachings at the White Horse Inn, and I threw myself into the proceedings as much as any other student. But eventually, it became too much."

"This is when you went to Gloucestershire, wasn't it?" asked Poyntz.

"To work for Sir John Walsh," Tyndale nodded, surprised by his host's recollection. "Have I told you this before?"

"It might not be common knowledge, but Sir John's wife, Lady Anne, was a Poyntz, so she is family."

Tyndale shook his head, amazed he had not realized this truth before. "How could I not have seen that? Ah well, yes. I was overwhelmed by my intellectual pursuits and needed to be elsewhere. It wasn't that Cambridge was a bad place. Far from it! But it was as if the hidden hand of Almighty God was sending me elsewhere so my spirit could breathe. I needed to think about what I was learning in a more remote place, and I wanted to learn Greek in order to understand the New Testament."

"And my kinsman was a good employer?"

"He is wealthy and so giving me gainful employment was no difficulty," Tyndale acknowledged. "The true difficulty was what I discovered during my time there. I have spoken of this to several people, but never—I think—to you."

Poyntz remained quiet and Tyndale continued. "I was developing views that I realized were biblical and also opposite to the Roman Church. That was no surprise. But I still believed the best about those with whom I disagreed. I trusted they were scholars of Scripture and knowledgeable about God's revelation. Sir John would often have priests, and even the local bishop on occasion, to his house to break bread, and I would be at table with them, eating the meal but also conversing with them about their command of eternal truth."

"And from your demeanor now," said Poyntz, "I assume you were disappointed?"

"I will never forget the evening Sir John and Lady Anne hosted a Catholic priest. The roasted pork was excellent; the conversation less so. I confronted him for his appalling lack of knowledge about Scripture, to which he claimed as long as the pope declared his own word, it would be enough for the church. I gripped the table and charged that would not sustain the followers of Jesus Christ, to which he bellowed, 'We would be better without God's laws than those of the pope!'"

"I am surprised you survived any bouts of indigestion from that," Poyntz remarked.

"An upset stomach I could navigate," Tyndale scowled, "but his words I could not accept. I stood at the table and shook my finger at him and declared, '*Then I defy the pope and all his laws! And if God will see fit to spare my life for many years, I will cause a farm boy who pushes a plough to know more of the Scriptures than you do*!' I was shaking with anger, for I knew we could not transform England with such priestly ignorance. And yet, I also shook with hope, for if God is truly God, He would make a way to shine the light of His Word into the language of the people for their good and for His glory!"

They were turning into the lane toward Poyntz's home, and the grocer quietly said, "Then we must pray for the time you need to provide all of God's Word for the English people. And to that end, we must keep you safe!"

"Safety is in the hand of God," Tyndale responded, "and whether I live or die, His Word will go forth. That, my friend, is the gift that flows from the heart of our Lord and Savior."

Called "the apostle of England" by John Foxe, **WILLIAM TYNDALE** energized the Reformation in England with his translation of the Bible into the English language. Learning Hebrew and Greek so that he could translate Scripture from its original languages, Tyndale became a Protestant outlaw, on the run from King Henry VIII, who had declared any Bible but those in Latin illegal. Living on the European continent in places like Marburg, Hamburg, and Antwerp, Tyndale labored faithfully in producing the English New Testament (initially smuggled into England in 1526 in bales of cloth) and large portions of the Old Testament. In the end, Tyndale was betrayed by none other than Harry Phillips, who was employed by the Bishop of London and arranged for Tyndale's capture. Before being burned to death in October 1536, Tyndale pleaded, "Lord, open the eyes of the King of England." Years later, King Henry reversed his position and ordered English Bibles placed in every church in the land.

MARTIN BUCER

February 1537; Strasbourg, Holy Roman Empire

Snow was falling at a rapid pace as the wind howled through the streets of the city. Scowling in the midst of the gale, Martin Bucer pushed forward toward the cathedral, where he saw his friend Caspar Hedio opening the great front doors. Increasing his pace, Bucer waved at a passerby before sprinting the final yards to the cathedral, and he was extremely happy when Hedio shut the door.

"You appear to have faced this day expecting the chill and snow from the heavens," Hedio remarked, taking Bucer's coat as his friend shook himself and vigorously rubbed his hands to bring the warmth back to them. Feeling the blood coursing through his fingers once again, Bucer waggled his head, clearing the snowflakes from his hair.

"As long as I live, I will see many winter squalls come suddenly upon this city," Bucer muttered. "It is a shame the mountains of the Vosges and Black Forest do not buffet the piercing cold wind! It's not so much the snow that I mind as this blasted wind."

"Consider this," Hedio said as they walked up the center aisle toward the pulpit where Hedio spent so many of his Sundays as the great church's preacher, "the wind can be a blessing."

"And how is that?" asked Bucer.

"It's a reminder you are still alive, and if you are alive," Hedio paused with a flourish, "then it means our Lord has work for you to do in His name."

Bucer allowed a smile. "You are correct, friend, although I could do with something warm to ensure that I stay alive."

"This way," Hedio pointed toward the side door. "I do have some beef stew in my study if you fancy that."

The stew, made by Hedio's wife Margareta, was excellent, and Bucer was all the more glad there was a supply of crusty bread for dipping. The stew warmed Bucer's insides and blunted his hunger as he had not eaten anything all day.

"A pleasant offering from your bride, Caspar," Bucer said. "Of course, she grants you joy beyond meals."

"A godly and skilful wife is a gift from God," Hedio agreed. "Nearly thirteen years of joy now. You know plenty of that, too, Martin, although your marriage seems all the more radical."

"Elisabeth has often said a life with me has been more of a change than she could ever imagine," Bucer agreed.

"Because you practically snatched her from a convent which caused her to break all her vows of chastity, poverty, and obedience!" Hedio guffawed. "Ah well, you showed yourself to be a judge of good women, Martin. And by marrying her, you were willing to face the church's response so that many of us could reap the same benefits."

"It is so remarkably striking," Bucer mused, "that such action has marked us as so different from Rome. I sometimes wonder that our Catholic counterparts would be less shocked if we desecrated a cathedral than be pastors who took wives."

"Some might believe they are the same thing," said a voice from the doorway.

"Wolfgang, hello!" said Bucer to their visitor, the theologian and teacher Wolfgang Capito. "We are here reminiscing about how earth-shaking our marriages have been to our opponents."

"I am late to such a competition," said Capito, "but Wibrandis has made me a very happy man." He stopped, looking at the stew and then Bucer. "Which brings me here, Martin. I am concerned."

"Concerned?" said Bucer and Hedio together.

"Not by that stew," Capito answered. "No, I am perplexed because you look wearied, as if the weight of the world has been on your shoulders."

"We all carry weight on our shoulders, Wolfgang," said Bucer.

"We do indeed," Capito replied, "but lately you seem more overcome than normal."

"Have you been keeping things from me, Martin?" said Hedio in a poor attempt at humor to quell the heaviness of spirit.

"No," Bucer said, sighing and stretching. "I think it is too much over the past ten years. I sense my spirit being frayed over so much activity. Good work, mind you, but difficult to sustain."

"You have us by your side, my friend," acknowledged Capito.

"Yes, and for that I am grateful, but I am still aware of my great shortcomings," Bucer replied. "We had such a grand opportunity to unite ourselves with our friend Zwingli and with Luther himself, and yet we could not broker a way forward at Marburg because Luther would not budge on Holy Communion. *This is my body.* He would not let go of a literal understanding. I don't begrudge him that, but walking out meant we were more divided than united against Rome."

"You could not be expected to have done more, Martin," said Hedio kindly. "You were negotiating, not performing magic."

"And there is this long, drawn out affair with the re-baptizers who moved into our city years ago," Bucer recalled. "We must always be welcoming to those fleeing persecution. But some among them sought to take over Strasbourg. They call into question any idea of a true Christian community when they separate church from the rest of life. We apply our faith to our entire community, for we live amongst each other. They tend to make it highly personal and individual, and forget about others. And yet my heart is warmed by their passion. How I desire to find some common ground with them."

"I believe we've had those debates with them many times over, Martin," Capito cautioned, "and I think we can live together with them in spite of our disagreements."

"We baptize infants, the ones who move into our midst often refuse to," added Hedio. "A significant conviction, much like some other differences, but must these issues divide us when we are truly together in Christ?"

"No," said Bucer. "I just wonder how much strength I have remaining for more challenges. It seems that many of us are facing difficulties. I hear from Geneva that Calvin and Farel might be expelled. As sad a day that would be for Geneva, we could use someone of Calvin's ability here."

"We truly do not know what is ahead," said Capito. "All we can do is trust our Savior Christ."

The three men nodded in agreement, but suddenly their heads turned as they heard the door of the cathedral fly open with devastating force. Hearing the clatter of feet in the church, the three men leapt to their feet and headed in the direction of the noise, only to come face to face with a pack of Strasbourg tower guards near the Communion table.

"Masters Bucer, Capito, and Hedio," their captain gasped. "We have failed to find any of you in your homes and only now have we managed to discover you here. Please! You must come quickly!"

"To where?" Bucer pleaded, his jaw set and heart racing.

"With us," the captain replied. "Come with us to the Porte de Saverne. Quickly!"

The city gate on the north side of Strasbourg remained closed, granting relief from the howling wind as Bucer and his friends approached along with the captain. Bucer blew on his hands as the plunging temperatures brought significant discomfort.

"Here, sir," another soldier hailed the captain. "We are waiting upon you to order the opening of the gate."

Turning to Bucer, the captain held out a stiff arm. "Take care, Master Bucer. We're about to open the Saverne's door."

"And what is on the other side?" asked Bucer, who heard clamor from the other side of the wall.

"Not what. Who," shouted the captain, who roared an order to his subordinates to unlatch the great door.

"Caspar," Bucer said, taking the cathedral preacher by the elbow. "Make haste to the Zell house and tell Matthias to be ready with food, water, blankets, and any other supplies."

"What do you mean, Martin?"

"I have a settled conviction God is bringing these people into our care," Bucer replied. "Hurry!" And Hedio scampered down the avenue. "Wolfgang," he turned to Capito, "follow my lead."

The door swung open, bringing a blast of chilly air from the outside of the gate. Bucer looked through the opening and saw in the distance the slow-moving waters of the frost-ridden Rhine. However, the river was not what truly caught his attention. There, shivering in the snow, skin pale and lips blue from the cold and exposure, were what seemed like two hundred people, their shabby clothes barely covering their bodies. Bucer, his heart pounding with compassion, pushed past the guards and entered the crowd.

"We look for the man of Saint Thomas!" rasped a man near the front of the bedraggled column lurching into the city. "Can anyone tell me where he is?" And the traveler promptly burst into tears.

"My good man," Bucer called out, slipping on the snow-laden stones while attempting to steady his new visitor's steps. "I am Martin Bucer, the minister at Saint Thomas' Church. Please come into the city, and perhaps we can find you a space to warm yourselves!"

"We haven't searched them for weapons, Master Bucer!" the captain warned.

"Good captain," Bucer shot back, "I think we can assume they have not come to attack us!"

"Agreed," added Capito, "because with this band being more than half children, I doubt they would be smuggling swords."

Bucer looked into the eye of the stranger who had addressed him. He saw weariness in the man's face. Skin was stretched over cheekbones, and he bore a cut on his left jaw. Two children were clinging to his side, a boy and a girl, neither of which—Bucer judged—could be more than eight years of age. The man's balding head was crowned with a stubborn patch of hair, a mix of chestnut and grey.

"My friend," Bucer began, "what is your name and from where have you come?"

"Master Bucer," replied the man in a voice that was thick and husky from his recent sobs, "my name is Etienne. With me are my children Gulliaume and Jeanette, and what remains of the community of the

Reformed faith in Chaumont. We have come on foot for the past four days after our expulsion by order of the authorities. My shop was burned to the ground with my dear wife still inside! Farms of my fellow believers were ravaged. We were told to be gone by sundown three days ago or we would be killed!"

"By King Francis?" The question was from Capito, who was incredulous.

"Henchmen, local soldiers ... Does it matter?" And Etienne's knees buckled as he wept the words.

"Etienne!" Bucer exclaimed in pity. "My friend, my brother in Christ, be welcome here!" He saw Etienne in the grasp of his son and immediately caught him in a fierce embrace. "Etienne, how many made this journey with you?"

"Fifteen dozen, sir," said little Jeanette. And we haven't eaten since breakfast yesterday."

"An injustice that we shall remedy now," replied Bucer, turning to Capito. "Wolfgang?"

"To the church? Yes," his friend nodded. "And I'll go round to the houses of the council and inform them."

"And while you are doing that," Bucer implored him, "ask our wives to bring all the food we can manage."

In the nave of Saint Thomas' Church, Bucer and his wife moved among the huddled, shivering throng that now sat digesting beef and vegetable stew that they believed fit for a king. The other pastors had joined them, assisted by their families, bringing bread to those who asked and filling mugs with warm beer, designed to help stave off the severe chills of the travelers. Their widened eyes told the entire story: They never dreamed today they would be served a delicious meal in the middle of a church.

When all had been served, Bucer stood in their midst. As he did, he prayed silently, *Help me, Holy Spirit. I do not know where this might lead, but if these are your people escaping persecution, help this church and this city to be sanctuaries in their time of deep distress.* All assembled grew quiet, waiting for his announcement.

"I wish to assure all of you," he began, "that this meal and this rest is no mere pause before starting your travels once again. My fellow pastors and I have spent the last half hour discussing your plight with the members of our city council, and we wish to extend this invitation of hope to all of you, that you are most welcome to stay here and make Strasbourg your home, your peace, your refuge from the terrible anguish that you have endured. Regarding your needs, your employment, and your shelter, we will seek to find all you require so you may dwell among us in security."

The gasps of happiness shot through the church, and many of the refugees fell to their knees, weeping openly. Etienne stumbled toward Bucer and spoke loudly so all could hear.

"My dear friend," he stammered, "we are so grateful. This morning we awoke as hunted prey, and now you give us a home. You are indeed an answer to prayer. But why?"

Bucer kindly laid his hand on Etienne's shoulder and looked around at all of Strasbourg's new residents. "When our Lord Jesus was a baby and it was necessary to leave Bethlehem to escape the sword of Herod, his family went to Egypt, a place that was not their home, to receive safety and all they required at that time. What we can do for you, Etienne, and your fellow travelers, we do for Christ Himself!"

All in the church began lifting praises to God for the miracle given, to which Bucer smiled warmly and declared, "And if Etienne has said we are an answer to prayer, it is appropriate we give our offering of thanks to the King of Heaven who has brought you to us!"

They stood together, and Bucer prayed, his words lyrical, his tone full of music and grace: "Almighty God, heavenly Father, we give You eternal praise and thanks that You have been so gracious unto us poor sinners, having drawn us to Your Son our Lord Jesus, whom You have delivered to death for us and given to be our nourishment and our dwelling unto eternal life. Grant that we may never relinquish these things from our hearts, but ever grow and increase in faith to You, which, through love, is effective of all good works. And so, may our whole life be devoted to Your praise and the edification of our neighbor; through the same Jesus Christ, our Lord. Amen."

The legacy of **MARTIN BUCER** encompasses many descriptions: reformer, teacher, pastor, and generous friend. His work in Strasbourg solidified the Reformation and the doctrines of grace in a major city in Europe. His relationships with church leaders from many countries enabled him to have influence in Lutheran, Calvinist, and Anglican churches. A deep thinker and earnest churchman, Bucer wrote liturgies to be used during worship in Strasbourg's churches and he exhibited a gracious approach to engaging with both friends and religious opponents. Leaving Strasbourg late in life, he journeyed to England, where he joined with Thomas Cranmer in establishing the Reformation on British shores, and assisting in the revision of the Book of Common Prayer.

FACT FILES

Reformers Behind the Scenes

There is a danger in studying history. Very often, we are drawn to the most significant leaders and shapers of world events. This is entirely understandable. We tend to notice what is most visible. If you are outdoors in a grassy area inhabited by dogs, you would likely see bouncy Welsh corgis and lumbering bulldogs but would likely have to strain to see grasshoppers hidden in the grass.

The same tendency exists in church history. Our eyes tend to be on the major players who led great movements, but we also need to recognize the great importance of others who supported leaders or began a course of action that was completed by future leaders. They might not be as well-known as a Martin Luther, a John Calvin, or a Thomas Cranmer, but they deserve a noted place in our study.

Many years before the English Reformation began, the writings of Luther found fertile soil in the hearts of university students in England. Thomas Bilney (1495-1531) was a Cambridge scholar who led a group of fellow students in studying the New Testament in its original Greek text. In the early 1500s, he happened upon a number of Luther's writings and became convinced that one is justified by God's grace through faith. He was particularly struck by I Timothy 1:15, in which the apostle Paul wrote, "Christ Jesus came into the world to save sinners, of whom I am the foremost." This news of Jesus' sacrifice for him brought Bilney's heart a great deal of peace, for he was no longer subject to wondering if he had done enough to earn God's salvation; the truth that Christ had paid for his sins in His death comforted him greatly. In no time, Bilney's passion and influence won over his friends, some of whom—like Matthew Parker and Hugh Latimer—would become leaders when the English Reformation gathered full strength. Preaching against saints and holy relics, and fervently proclaiming the doctrines of salvation by grace through faith in Christ, Bilney was eventually removed from the pulpit of St. George's, Ipswich, and imprisoned in the Tower of London. Released when he swore not to preach as he had, he felt deep guilt over his promise and instead openly preached the biblical ideas of Luther all the more. Finally, he was arrested in Norwich and tried for heresy. This time, he gladly accepted a martyr's death when burned at the stake in August 1531, in a calm spirit that impressed even his Catholic opponents.

Though John Calvin receives much credit for the Reformation in Geneva, Switzerland, one cannot overlook the impact of William Farel (1489-1565). He was a Frenchman who, as we have seen earlier, was mentored by Jacques Lefévre d'Étaples, but intense persecution forced Farel to leave his homeland of France and make his way to Bern, Switzerland. As Bern was supporting the city of Geneva in its bid for independence from the Italian province of Savoy, Farel went to Geneva in an attempt to convince the churches of Geneva to adopt the emerging Protestant convictions. Farel labored sincerely as a pastor in Geneva, but he faced two challenges. One was that while Geneva was more accepting of the Protestant faith, this was mainly due to a desire to be free from Catholic Italy rather than by a concern for what was biblical or not. The other challenge lay in Farel's own approach. He was a tall, authoritative figure with flaming red hair and a booming voice. His fiery commands for repentance were well-heard, but he lacked the ability to carefully guide a movement to gradually persuade an entire city toward a biblical approach to life. When Farel discovered that John Calvin was staying in Geneva for a night in 1536, he came to the place where Calvin was lodging and demanded he stay and help him implement the Reformation in Geneva. Calvin tried to beg Farel off, claiming he was on his way north-eastward to Strasbourg for a quiet ministry of writing and teaching. But Farel was unmoved. He stood over Calvin and berated him for desiring his own quiet life over the spiritual needs of the people of Geneva, declaring that God would curse his life's efforts if he turned his back on that city. Moved by Farel's passion (and perhaps afraid of what a man twice his size might do to him!), Calvin relented and remained in Geneva. After both men were expelled from Geneva (see the next chapter on Calvin), Farel left to become a pastor in Neuchatel, but he and Calvin maintained a lifelong friendship and correspondence. Without Farel's initiative, there would have been no Reformation under Calvin in Geneva.

The fire and passion of William Farel was not far from the colorful personality of Martin Luther in Germany. Luther had the giftedness and heart ablaze to launch a Reformation. Yet God also saw fit to raise up others who could continue the Reformation in Germany and teach the next generation with skill and patience. Phillip Melanchthon (1497-1560) was the careful teacher who could connect with others, making things simple and clear to inquirers, to continue what Luther had begun. To this effect, Melanchthon wrote *Loci Theologica,* a theology text used to train Lutheran pastors. Even Luther himself knew that their opposites in temperament were part of God's plan to expand the Reformation in Germany. Luther said he was a "rowdy and stormy" soul who fought against enemies of the Gospel, but that God had granted Melanchthon a different nature, marked by stability, calm, and gentleness, that could establish God's truth in Germany, "sowing and watering with joy." Even though he and Luther did not agree on every single point, Melanchthon's wide-ranging abilities brought a human touch to his teaching, and he was able to forge friendships with other churchmen and reformers beyond the orbit that Luther could make.

Another great contributor to the Protestant cause was an Italian named Peter Martyr Vermigli (1499-1562). This Augustinian monk began reading works by Ulrich Zwingli and Martin Bucer (discussed previously) and was mentored by a humanist scholar named Juan de Valdes. Vermigli's desire to proclaim the Reformers' teachings in his monastery brought him into conflict with his superiors, and he fled to Strasbourg in the Holy Roman Empire, where he and Bucer became close friends and where Vermigli taught Old Testament. Later, Thomas Cranmer invited Vermigli to come to England and help with the Reformation that had launched the Anglican Church there. In the midst of these moves, Vermigli had become a prodigious writer who combined careful biblical study with his respect for ancient philosophy and logic. He wrote many commentaries on books of the Bible, his work on the Epistle to the Romans receiving highest praise. Another work, known as *Loci Communes,* was a collection made of a vast number of his quotes from his books. Arranged by doctrinal topics, it became an influential favorite of many Reformed thinkers. He also was devoted to the place of Holy Communion in Christian worship, believing that the Lord's Supper showed the union of Jesus with His people through the work of the Holy Spirit.

One matter to keep in mind during the Reformation was how critical the presence of women was to its labor in a male-dominated world. Luther and Calvin relied on the inner strength and godliness of their wives, Katie and Idelette, respectively. Anne Boleyn, the second wife of King Henry VIII, never gave him a male heir (though she did bear a daughter who became Queen Elizabeth I), but her keen interest in church matters positioned her to suggest the names of Thomas Cranmer, Hugh Latimer, and Nicholas Ridley, among others, to places of leadership that would ignite the English Reformation. One other woman was used greatly by God in central Europe. Although Matthew Zell helped start the Reformation in Strasbourg in 1521 with his preaching at the Saint Laurence chapel, his wife Katerina is likely even more well known for her efforts. For one, she was amongst the first Protestant women to marry a minister. Supportive of Matthew's preaching and pastoring throughout their twenty-five-year marriage until his death in 1548, Katerina was known for her writings and her strong beliefs. Her tender heart for the care of others was a large part of her reputation. She wrote a large number of pamphlets on various doctrinal issues and commented on the work of the Reformation in that region. She was also a great encourager for those going through times of distress, one example being her treasured *Letter to the Suffering Women of Kentizingen,* where one reads words such as these:

> *God wants to show you, and those who come after you, and all of us, that you believe and that He loves you.*
>
> *Dear sisters, even though sometimes your faith may be discouraged, and the flesh may fight against the spirit, do not therefore be frightened away. It is a holy struggle; it must be thus: faith that is not tempted is not faith ... God will also not reckon what you do as impatience, if only the spirit does not remain under the flesh or the flesh overcome the spirit. Therefore, you should constantly pray to the Father, "Lord, help my unbelief"...*
>
> *So, dear Christian women, I cannot comfort and exhort you more and better now than to counsel you to accept such suffering with right patience and spiritual joy, for these are the fruits of the Spirit—so that God may be glorified in you above all others who are called, those who may not yet have been so greatly tried as you are. Consider the words of Christ ... He exhorts you and all His own to accept such things with patience and love.*

Although many who labored for the Protestant cause are not as well-known as Martin Luther, John Calvin, or Thomas Cranmer, we benefit greatly from the godly and humble efforts of many of these "reformers behind the scenes."

JOHN CALVIN

September 1541, Geneva, Switzerland

Heaving the weighty door open, the diminutive man shuffled out of the drafty chamber into the sanctuary. An awed hush settled upon the assembly that gathered in the candlelit interior of Saint Pierre's Church, broken only by a stray cough or a toddler's warble. Every watchful eye in the entire room alighted upon the short form that stepped gingerly up the staircase into the pulpit that hovered above the congregation that held its collective breath. Even from his vantage point, the man could sense the questions roiling in their hearts.

Does he come to condemn us? What words of blame will he speak? How can he ever forgive us?

Stifling a cough, the smallish figure lifted his foot over the last step and stood resolutely behind the pulpit's lectern. What history there had been between him and this city. His eyes swept over the congregation and took in the looks of all assembled. Bakers. Artisans. Schoolteachers. Woodworkers. Millers. Clothiers. And so many more. Among the lot were the members of the city council. And that brought back the memories, pushing into his heart like a plow into the soft earth. John Calvin briefly closed his eyes. And remembered back to three years before.

"You, Master Calvin, minister at St. Pierre's, and you, Master Farel of St. Gervais," boomed the haughty voice of the city meister in the warm chamber, "along with Master Corault are brought before us due to your wanton refusal to heed our commands for the good of the life of our fair city!"

"What is the charge?" bellowed the deep-chested William Farel. "Or have you not gotten your stories aligned at this point? Is it because we will not submit to the worship demands of Bern? Or because we retain the right to fence the table of our Lord's Communion?"

"Silence!" the city meister shot back, rapping his gavel-club on the desk before him for good measure. "You will submit to this council. The churches of Geneva come into our oversight as part of the city; the city is not part of the churches. You are to desist from preaching in your churches or you will be forced from this city! And then you will know what true terror might be."

"Tell me, respected one," Calvin spoke firmly but gently. "How is expulsion from Geneva for following Christ to be true terror? How is that to be any worse than what we endure now and will endure once we leave this chamber, when the mob will surely come upon us in the street, spitting upon us and hissing in our faces, beating us with sticks and firing gunshots at our windows at night, all the while chanting to throw us into the Rhone as they sing their obscene songs about the Supper of our Lord?" Calvin felt Corault press against him, the blind preacher whimpering more out of sadness than fear. He continued, "Tell me how expulsion shall be worse, if we only would follow our Savior?"

That had been his bold reply to the council. It was certainly less harrowing than the walk home that night, buffeted on all sides by the jeering population of Geneva who had tired of Calvin's calls to repentance and faith.

Calvin stood in the pulpit, looking out at the congregation once more, their anger of the previous three years changed to soft entreaty for kind words of hope. He gripped the pulpit, as he remembered gripping it on that fateful Easter Sunday soon after the council's warning thirty-nine months before.

"And to that end," he preached then, "there shall be no celebration of the Lord's Supper this day in St. Pierre's. Nor can you run across the river to St. Gervais and expect bread and wine from the hand of Farel, for he is giving the same message within those walls!" Calvin's sad eyes bored into the hearts of the people in the church. "How indeed can you mock the Lord Himself and sin so grievously against Christ crucified by your looting, jeering, and rioting, and with those same hands reach forth for His meal? None of you," Calvin spoke in measured anger, "shall receive the life-giving victuals of Christ Himself. God forbid we celebrate His Holy Supper awash in your rebellion!"

That week, they had been called again to the city chamber, where the council rendered their judgment. With haughty looks from the leaders who peered down from their chairs, the herald announced the sentence: "Masters Calvin, Corault, and Farel, this council finds you guilty of civic disorder and rebellion for your prideful and deliberate disobedience of their express desire. They, not you, determine who is worthy to receive from Christ's Table. Therefore, we give you no greater than three days to remove yourselves from our city. Where you may seek shelter or occupation from then on is your concern, not ours."

Farel stepped forward, his face flaming as red as his hair, but Calvin stayed him with a firm grip on his sleeve and a shake of his head. In the end,. it was Calvin to move forward and speak his parting word.

"This is indeed to our health and goodness," he remarked, "for it would be a pathetic payment if we were serving the princes of men. Yet it is a fine reward for us, for our Master is true, kind, and faithful, and in His name we will go."

Calvin looked out again from the pulpit to the people of Geneva, even as the distant memory of his expulsion remained. The congregation desired a word from him, but more importantly, they required God's Word. That was all that mattered now, not the memories of exile or the questions that pulsed through his heart when they begged for his return.

"Let us pray," Calvin began as they bowed their heads as one. "Holy Savior, we beseech you upon this Lord's Day to receive our praises, feeble though they be, and to take our trembling prayers into your friendly heart. Only by Your sovereign hand may we place any hope in the restoration of our world. We come before You praying for the safety of Your followers and all within the land of Hungary as the Turks seek to break down the walls of Budapest. For the sick and suffering in Germany, we lift up our prayers and ask You relieve them of the ravages of plague and death. In France, our brothers and sisters in the faith face the daily horror of persecution and affliction. May we humble ourselves before You, O our God. We pray for the world and for our fellow believers under heavy duress and the point of death. And may You, Lord God Almighty, have mercy upon our city even now, and take us under the gentle and kind wings of Your protection. Amen."

Calvin found himself remembering his time in Strasbourg. *The wings of my Savior's protection,* Calvin wept as he sat with the letter spread in front of him on his desk. Never did he imagine this entreaty would pierce his heart, let alone come to him. *Why is it,* he asked his Lord in prayer, *that when I have ministry so profitable and wondrous and blessed that You send the needs of others to intrude upon my happiness?*

He had been in Strasbourg for three happy years. Coming at the invitation of his friend Martin Bucer, Calvin had found a church populated with French refugees in need of comfort and patient teaching of the Scriptures. Into this work, Calvin had thrown himself with vigor, finding such joy in the small, huddled assembly of his fellow French comrades. He found at last the time for writing he desired. He penned a number of biblical psalms and the Apostles' Creed set to music. His *Institutes of the Christian Religion* had gone to the printer a second time, this time translated by Calvin himself into his native French language. His lectures on Paul's letter to the Romans was printed and published. He enjoyed his teaching opportunity at the nearby school, wrote an additional book on worship, and found time to visit his church members in their homes to pray and read Scripture with them. And—blessing of all—he even found a wife! His dear Idelette had warmed his heart and made him happier than he believed possible.

And now that happiness was under threat, or so Calvin thought, with the urgings of the letter from Geneva's Council before him practically reaching up to choke him from the page. In clear script, the words came together as Calvin cleared his tears away:

Our good brother and special friend, we commend ourselves very affectionately to you ... we pray very earnestly that you would return to us, and return to your old place for former ministry where, we hope, by God's help, it will bring fruitful increase of the Holy Gospel. For our people greatly desire that you should live among us again, and they will act accordingly, so you will be content in your work.

Calvin shook his head. *What? Don't they recall how they treated me?* He had already shown the letter to his wife and was surprised that she didn't condemn the idea out of hand! He ended up taking the letter to his trusted friends in Strasbourg, who surprised him with their contentment in God's will. One was particularly direct: "Of course we want you to stay in Strasbourg, Master Calvin, given what a delight you have been to us and to the Gospel of Jesus Christ among us. But, if this request from Geneva originates from the very heart and will of our Lord and Savior, how can we dare stand in His way?"

Even Idelette was willing to go with her husband wherever God may send him. "Oh, my wife," Calvin would complain, "going back to Geneva would be like dying daily a thousand times over." "Then I shall go with you and be there for every death and every time the Lord shall, in His mercy, raise you up," she replied.

He shall raise me up, thought Calvin as he resolved to accept the offer to return to Geneva. *Then in Christ I shall place my trust.*

Even as the prayer ended in St. Pierre's, Calvin could sense the anxiety and tension throughout the sanctuary, thick as the snow that fell in the surrounding areas in winter. Calmly, he opened his Bible as the worshipers held their breath. He knew what they were thinking. *The ending of the prayer can open the door to a sermon of scorn and blame.* He knew they were expecting a tongue-lashing, one they believed they and the city fully deserved. *But if I give them rebuke for the past, he thought, how can I expect to demonstrate consistently the grace of Jesus in their midst?* He paged through his Bible until he came to the passage, the one he had been about to preach on three years previously, before that phlegmatic pony carried him off to Strasbourg.

He looked up from his Bible, and smiling, he raised his hands heavenward.

"I ask that we, of one heart and one faith, all stand for the reading of the Word of God!"

As he read, he could sense both the relief and the joy circulate amongst those assembled in St. Pierre's! Relief that he held no grudge against them; joy that the Word of Christ was being preached faithfully to them! It was the exact verse where he had stopped preaching when he had been unjustly forced out. He was on to the next thing the Lord desired to set before them. They had Calvin back, and he looked to the present and the future, not their past!

It was at breakfast the next day that Calvin sat next to his beautiful Idelette at their long pine table where they would sit for meals in their house on Canon Street. His head was clouded from a night of little sleep, but Idelette noticed something even more encouraging. His eyes were dancing in spite of his weariness. Her husband had barely dragged himself out of bed, but his eyes were full of life!

"And how does it feel to be back, my darling?" Idelette asked him.

Calvin smiled broadly. "I never thought I would say this, my love, but I am encouraged. Yes, there will be much to set right and many details to which I must attend. But I find this strangely refreshing. If I have much work before me, that is much work that the Lord, by His grace, might make fruitful."

It was then that they both jumped at a sharp rapping at the door. Idelette managed to reach it first and turned the handle, revealing a husband, wife, son, and daughter. Calvin eased himself next to his wife and looked out into the morning sunlight and then down at the little girl before taking in the whole family.

"Jakob, Margareta!" he exclaimed before stooping down to greet the children. "Claude and Gretel!" He saw the colorful stalk in Gretel's hands as the child grinned at him. "Oh Gretel," he chortled, "have you brought me some deep blue gentians?"

"I have," Gretel giggled, suddenly jumping forward and embracing Calvin fiercely, "but you may have them only if you promise you will stay!"

Joining the laughter of both families, Calvin reached down and picked Gretel up into his arms. "Do you know, dear one?" he replied. "You've won my heart. I promise you."

No one had a more magnificent impact on the spread of the Reformation than **JOHN CALVIN**. A student of law and then the priesthood, Calvin traveled from his home in France with the intention of quiet study and writing in Strasbourg in 1536, but William Farel detained him with the great need to reform the city of Geneva and align it to biblical devotion. Although they were expelled in 1538, Calvin accepted Geneva's offer of a return and came back to the city in 1541 as pastor of St. Pierre's Church. In addition, he founded the Geneva Academy, which trained ministers from all over Europe to return to their lands and spread the Reformed faith. A respected writer, Calvin also produced commentaries on books of the Bible, his *Institutes of the Christian Religion*, many confessions of faith and worship resources, and preached over two thousand sermons during his ministry in Geneva. Determined to shape peoples' lives according to the Gospel, Calvin lived by a simple and profound vision: To God alone the glory.

CATHERINE PARR

July 1544; Windsor Castle, England

"Your Majesty!" called out the servant, his slight form bouncing in his horse's saddle as he turned toward the queen and her companions in the carriage. "Since we are about ten minutes from the castle, I can ride ahead and announce your coming presence if you so desire!"

So eager was the servant that he nearly slipped from his horse, catching himself in time and heaving several deep breaths into his stocky frame as his face grew red in the summer heat. The horse-drawn carriage which he approached drew to a halt at the coachman's order. Slowly leaning toward the open window frame and graciously making no comment on the servant's clumsiness, a fair-skinned, dark-haired woman beamed a reassuring smile.

"Thank you, Thomas," she said. "We will be well-protected with the remainder of our guard. If you could please ask His Majesty to meet with me in the gardens, I would be grateful to you."

Tipping his cap and bowing slightly, Thomas wheeled his horse around and began a dash westward. The carriage began moving forward again, and, drawing back into her seat, Catherine Parr, Queen of England and Ireland, gave a weary sigh.

"Given your late nights reading and writing, m'lady," said the young woman across from her, "I am surprised you have not chosen to nap the entire journey from Richmond!"

The queen's eyes shone, suddenly sparkling with renewed energy at the mention of her evening labors. "It is true I have burned many candles over the past month, dear Lucy, but I am not sleepy. Somewhat tired, yes. But God gives sleep to me when I require it. My business today is much more urgent, so my Lord shall sustain me with the health and strength that comes graciously from His hand."

"And given that you brought along many sheaves of your inscriptions, one might justly assume that you are to share them with the king?" asked her companion seated at her side.

"Some in particular, good Margaret," Queen Catherine replied. "Not all, for I know he would like to leave with his army by the end of the year!" She smiled at her attempt at humor. "I have been thinking intently ... No, that is not the proper word. I have been considering prayerfully what to bring to his ears this day. I am very emotional about his departure for France, and given that it is with his army, the chance exists these could be the last moments we spend together."

"I have heard the news is encouraging from France," said Lucy, "if the gossip of stable boys is anything to swear by."

"You should think quite highly of stable boys, Lucy," the queen noted, "for I would tend to believe what they said more than, say, the words of courtiers and political advisors. Those in the palace can often proclaim what they want you to believe; the humble of the earth give the truth unvarnished more often than we imagine."

"Is this why you speak so little to members of the King's Council?" inquired Margaret.

"I simply mean that truth is not the sole possession of the high and lofty," responded Queen Catherine, "but we find it in droves in the humble of the earth. They may be our servants, but they are also our teachers more than we might imagine."

The ladies sat quietly, digesting the words of their queen. Since she had appointed her stepdaughter Margaret

Neville as her lady-in-waiting and Lucy Somerset, her stepson John's wife, as her maid of honor, the two women had often remarked that conversation with Catherine was a rich education in itself. Although she did not brandish her views loudly and openly, both women acknowledged that the queen was a woman of deep wisdom and goodness who outranked almost every man they knew in those regards.

"I must confess, m'lady," began Margaret, "that when you married the king, I did not imagine this depth of devotion from you toward him. Please do not misunderstand me. This is not in regards to your character. But, in all confidence, his reputation was, dare I say, questionable."

"Thank you, Margaret," the queen answered, "and I know you were not speaking ill of me. There were times when I wondered if this was indeed what God desired of me. But I obeyed the king when he proposed marriage, and in spite of some differences, we have made a decent way forward the past year. I know that since I am the sixth wife he has had, any joy on my part would meet some detractors, but God has made it a good union."

"Although you are clearly siding with the thought of Luther and not with Rome?" asked Lucy.

"I side with where Scripture takes me, my good and dear maid," Catherine replied. "And I have meditated on this greatly in my late nights in the recent past. Why else would our Lord Jesus Christ be that Light of the world unless the darkness of sin and rebellion dwelt in our hearts from birth? Why would He be our Prince of Peace if there were no war between us and heaven? How could He be our Great Physician unless our souls are plagued with the fever and illness of sin which we cannot break by our best works?"

"Truly I have not seen anyone live with such confidence in that hope for so long, m'lady," replied Margaret.

"Because the grace of God is so starkly clear and glorious, when I see my wretchedness that places me in such need, I know Christ's mercies are the only security for me. Oh Margaret! Oh Lucy! There is no other place I could direct my hope. I could have confidence in nothing in heaven or earth, but in Christ, my true and only Savior! I come to Him, sick and grievously wounded, and he heals and restores me. I do not ask for bread, but for the crumbs that fall from His table, and yet He sets before me a delicious and satisfying feast of His goodness! I deserve to be cast into the fires of hell, yet He seeks me to save me, and because of His faithfulness, He is unwilling that I should be cast out of His presence! If I should look upon my sins and not the mercy of Christ poured out in His death on the Cross, I would only despair. But He appeased His Father in His death and sacrificed Himself for me. For me, my dear ladies!" The queen, undone by her emotion, sank back in her cushioned seat, joyful tears splashing from her eyes.

Several moments went by before the ladies spoke again, and by then they could see the form of Windsor Castle as it rose before them. "I do hope, m'lady," Lucy offered, "that this will not be the final meeting between you and the king."

"He goes to France to fight and lead as a soldier," said Queen Catherine, "and whatever occurs is out of my hands, but in God's. And my Savior has overcome death by His own death. Yes, if my lord the king should die, it would be hard. But what if we had to face it without Jesus' death?"

"I am certain, m'lady," said Margaret, "that you are not finished with your writings if these truths are what Almighty God has laid on your heart."

"Perhaps not," the queen replied, "but we are here and I must go to my husband. I will pray, though, that the same Jesus who opened my heart to receive salvation from Him will continually soften your hearts to His Word every day."

Thomas approached the carriage door and bowed. "Your Majesty, the king is in the gardens."

Catherine had Lucy and Margaret accompany her into the spacious gardens. Although Thomas had said the king would be spending a great deal of time here, it was several minutes before they discovered him. King Henry had hobbled a few feet away from the rosebushes and was smelling a collection of cornflowers when he looked up and saw his bride approaching him.

"My gracious and fair queen," Henry spoke, his voice quavering slightly, "it is good of you to come." He drew near Catherine, nodding politely to Lucy and Margaret, and surprised his wife when he placed his hand in hers. "May we sit together? I would suggest a walk, but this blasted leg would prevent me taking many steps."

"You are my king," Catherine replied. "Your wish is my pleasure."

On a nearby bench, they sat in companionable silence for several moments before Henry sighed and looked at the distant trees. "I am to depart tomorrow to take the road to Dover and join the remnants of our army on this side of the Channel. By August, we intend to be in France to subdue Boulogne for good."

"The siege is a success?" asked Catherine. She had been named regent[1] for when Henry would be in France, and she thought it helpful to know as much as possible about military matters.

"That is the news so far. Norfolk sends word that more men could insure victory. I am not worried about defeat." He stopped, gently squeezing the queen's hand. "I am worried about an untimely death."

"All death is untimely, my lord," she responded, placing her other hand on top of his. "It is not how this world was

1. Being regent meant that Catherine would govern England while Henry was away.

intended to be. Sin has caused it to be otherwise." She paused. She had to tread carefully with her husband. It was one thing for her, Archbishop Cranmer, Prince Edward, and others to hold unswervingly to the Protestant faith; it was another to be too public about it under Henry's authority.

"I think," Henry's voice called her back to the present, "that going away has forced me to take stock of my life, my dear. I have gained power, have a dynasty secured through Edward's succession after I die, have solidified support from the gentry, and have broken with Rome and now I rule over the Church of England. Yet I sometimes sense a great emptiness clutching at my soul."

"It might be emptiness," Catherine offered, "or it could merely be a passing shadow of the heart."

Henry clutched his leg and winced. Catherine looked at him, keeping silence and waiting for him to reply.

"I am not a good man, my queen, and you certainly know that," Henry continued, "but I know people who seek to treat me well, who are the ones who do good. My Archbishop Cranmer is one such soul. There are others. You, my bride, are such a light in the midst of my darkness, much of which I tend to create myself." "You should take courage from the words of Christ, my husband," Catherine said slowly, with much emotion.

Her husband winced, though whether his flinch was from Catherine's words or his ghastly physical pain who could tell. Many looked at the king and saw a lumbering, obese form dragging his feet and weathering an ulcerated wound. Catherine looked at him and saw her monarch and husband. *To love, to cherish, and to obey, till death we do part,* she thought. She stroked the top of his hand.

"I don't know," he finally groaned, "how comforting they might be. The Lord Christ would likely expose my sin to the light."

"It is precisely by doing the former that He shall do the latter, O king," Queen Catherine said soothingly. "The apostle Peter knew it well."

"I am hardly in the same realm as Peter," Henry grumbled, gritting his teeth.

"Neither would I make that claim for myself," Catherine admitted, "but you do remember the Scriptures when the Lord told the disciples to put their nets into the lake for a catch. Peter, ever resistant, ever the fisherman who knew better, said they had caught nothing, but he would take Jesus at His word. And their catch was then so numerous that Peter was overcome by his unbelief. He said to our Lord, 'Depart from me, Lord, for I am a sinful man!' Do you recall?"

"I do," Henry grunted.

"And then Jesus told Peter 'Do not be afraid, from now on you will be catching men.' From sin to comfort. He knew who Peter was. He also knew who he could become by grace."

"I do not doubt your knowledge of Scripture, my queen," Henry rasped, "but what does this have to do with me?"

"Because our Lord knows who you are, as you confessed to be," Catherine said, taking both the king's hands in her own, "and He knows who He can make you to be. Oh, my husband and king! Fight well, fight faithfully, and may the Savior of heaven give you protection on earth!"

Henry's eyes softened, glistening. Lucy and Margaret had drawn several paces away but were close enough to hear Catherine whisper, "So allow me to pray for you."

The heads of four people in that quiet space bowed together, and the queen began to pray:

"O Almighty King and Lord of Hosts, Who have appointed Your angels to minister in both war and peace; and Who granted Your servant David both courage and strength: Instruct and teach my husband the king's hands to battle, and make his arms strong like a bow of steel. O

King of Kings, Lord of Lords, and the Ruler of all Princes, who sees all on earth from your great throne, with favor look upon Henry, my king and husband. Renew him with the grace of the Holy Spirit, that he might seek Your will and walk in Your way. Supply him generously with Your heavenly gifts, grant him health, strengthen him to vanquish and overcome all his enemies; and if he dies, may he enter everlasting joy and peace, through Christ our Lord. Amen."

And Catherine opened her eyes to see her hands wet and shining, for her husband the king was crying.

The sixth and final wife of King Henry VIII, **CATHERINE PARR** was the Queen of England and Ireland from 1543 until her death at thirty-six years of age in 1548. Although Henry's character was checkered at best, Catherine proved to be both a faithful wife and devoted Protestant queen. Greatly influenced by Lutheran teachings, she embraced the Gospel of Christ and was a lucid defender of justification by faith alone. She worked to reconcile Henry with his daughters Mary and Elizabeth before his death in 1547, helped to oversee the education of Henry's son (and later king) Edward, and communicated her beliefs with a clarity and passion rarely seen in history. She published her *Prayers or Meditations* (the first published book in the English language written by a woman), as well as her classic work *The Lamentation of a Sinner,* in which she called readers troubled by their wanderings and rebellion to a firm and secure hope in Jesus Christ.

FACT FILES

Charles V: The Man God Used to Launch Three Reformations

Sometimes people in high levels of authority have the idea they are freely making decisions that have great impact on the future. It is true their actions might be extremely important, momentous, and substantial. But they might require a dose of humility. Great leaders might actually be playing a role they are designed to play more than directing the action around them. In 2 Kings 19, the Assyrian army has surrounded Jerusalem and God's people are now threatened by the enemy. The King of Assyria openly mocks King Hezekiah and the Jewish people, proclaiming they are doomed. Hezekiah asks the prophet Isaiah for wisdom and comfort, and the prophet tells him what God has revealed (with a bite of holy sarcasm) about the Assyrian threat.

"*Have you not heard that I determined it long ago? I planned from days of old what now I bring to pass, that you should turn fortified cities into heaps of ruins ...*" (2 Kings 19:25).

In other words, the Assyrian king thought he was mowing people down in conquest, but God says, "No, not exactly. You are a pawn in my plans and I am using you to accomplish my purposes until you are cast aside."

Powerful leaders are not used to hearing words like those from God; often, they are not even aware that their actions are merely carrying out all that God permits for His greater glory. And great leaders do this, shall we say, unintentionally. They can help the very movements they would ordinarily desire to eliminate.

And in the Protestant Reformation, we find that the three major locations of this great work of God—Germany, Switzerland, and England—were impacted by none other than a devout Roman Catholic, the Holy Roman Emperor, Charles V!

How did that happen, you ask? It is one thing to inadvertently help one group in one place, but three?

It began in 1530. Charles was asserting his royal authority over the various smaller kingdoms in the Holy Roman Empire. At this time, Germany did not yet exist as the nation we know today. The Holy Roman Empire covered territory in the Netherlands, the present-day Czech Republic (Bohemia), and many individual states in the region of Germany. Charles already disliked Martin Luther for much of the past decade. Luther had refused to give up his Protestant beliefs at his imperial trial in Worms in 1521, over which Charles had presided. Now Charles was wanting to impose his iron will over all the Germanic princes in his empire. Inviting them to the city of Augsburg in the spring of 1530, he asked them to discuss certain questions. Suspicious of Charles' motives, the Protestant princes allied themselves with Martin Luther, Phillip Melanchthon, Justus Jonas, and Johannes Bugenhagen, who wrote a document detailing the core convictions of the Lutheran faith one of the major forms of Protestantism. Presenting this draft at Augsburg to Charles, the princes did not know for sure how the emperor would react.

But there was an added complication. Charles needed the armies of these princes because his standing army and his lands were under threat. From the old lands of the Byzantine Empire, the Ottoman Turks were pushing into eastern Europe and threatening key cities such as Vienna. Charles wanted to halt this advance, but he needed men in large numbers to do so. Making a practical, strategic decision that showed a good bit of tolerance, Charles allowed the princes to give full freedom to this Protestant faith in their territories in exchange for their military help. And so, the Reformation in Germany went on.

While Charles had more direct contact with the Lutheran leaders, his influence on the Swiss Reformation was more distant, yet just as profound. In the summer of 1536, a certain John Calvin knew that as a devoted Protestant believer and leader, his safety in Catholic France was not guaranteed. Even after spending some time with various friends and visiting Italy, he wanted to find a place where he could study, write, and teach in a quieter environment. The twenty-seven-year-old Calvin sought to travel to Strasbourg in the Holy Roman Empire. But here Charles unwittingly intervened. He clashed with France and King Francis I. Calvin discovered many bloody battles were erupting in the path he intended to take toward his new home. Plus, military carts and weaponry were clogging the roads. Calvin decided to take a roundabout path, heading south to Lyons before heading east toward Geneva. There he made arrangements to stay one night in an inn before continuing his journey to Strasbourg the next day. But William Farel, the thundering preacher, found out about Calvin's presence (as mentioned in another Fact File in this book), and after intense urgings and arguments, he convinced Calvin to stay in Geneva. A war involving Charles caused Calvin to take a detour to Geneva. And the Reformation in Switzerland went on.

Finally, Charles had a great impact on the English Reformation. This matter is somewhat complicated because the English king, Henry VIII, did not prize the Protestant faith at all, even though leaders such as Thomas Bilney, William Tyndale, Thomas Cranmer, Hugh Latimer, and Nicholas Ridley were firm in their Protestant convictions of the Gospel of Christ. Henry was a practical man who desired to have a male heir to succeed him as king (at this point, England had not yet had a female monarch). His wife, Catherine of Aragon, had failed to give him a son who lived past infancy, and Henry began to wonder if his marriage was cursed. Catherine was the widow of his late elder brother Arthur, and Henry had received special permission from Pope Julius II in 1503 in taking her as his wife. Henry now thought that was the wrong move. He read Leviticus 18:16 as a condemnation for taking the widow of one's brother, and so now in the late 1520s, he asked the present pope, Clement VII, to reverse Julius' ruling and now give Henry permission to annul (somewhat like divorce, saying the marriage was never legitimate to begin with) his marriage to Catherine. Granted, Henry was now attracted to Catherine's lady-in-waiting, Anne Boleyn, and intended to marry her.

Now Henry believed that Clement might grant the annulment, but the pope decided against it for two key reasons. First, the Reformation was just getting underway in Germany, where Martin Luther declared the popes and the Catholic Church were not perfect and could make serious errors in their decisions. For Clement to give Henry permission to annul his marriage to Catherine, it would show two popes making contradictory rulings on the same issue, giving proof to what the Reformers claimed. Secondly, Charles V entered the picture. Why was this question so critical to Charles? Why would he be so offended if Henry got his way against Catherine? Well, Catherine of Aragon just happened to be Charles' aunt! She was family! Charles was coming to her defense and he let Pope Clement know in crystal-clear terms that if he gave Henry the permission the English king desired, then Clement would not be able to count on the military protection from Charles' imperial troops.

And rather than stifling the Reformation, Charles' hard-line declaration only pushed Henry to announce that the English Church would no longer be ruled by Rome. Instead, Henry would be the supreme leader of the Church of England! This did not mean that Henry was a faithful Protestant at all; in fact, given that he had a total of six wives and would get dissatisfied by several of his brides very easily, and he really wasn't very faithful to others. But this is when priests like Tyndale, Cranmer, and others like them patiently and carefully established the Protestant faith in the English Church. Charles' demand pushed Henry to say goodbye to Roman rule. And the Reformation in England went on.

So, there is a great mystery: Someone who would normally be against the spiritual renewal of the Reformation had a good bit to do with its advance, even when those actions were strategic, accidental, or overly stubborn. But this should encourage us even today. God can use anyone to accomplish His plans, even if they would normally oppose that purpose. A God Who is that sovereign and wise is surely One we should be willing to bow before, worship, serve, and love.

THOMAS CRANMER

January 27-28, 1547, London, England

"Of course, it is damp," declared Nicholas Ridley as he sauntered up the center aisle of St. Paul's Cathedral. "We've had nothing but rain and snow the past two weeks, the whole church is drafty, and the king has disbursed no funds to improve the look of the place. And it is evening. Hardly the time for a chance of warmth. Just these occasional gatherers gossiping about the latest news."

"Ah, Master Ridley," rejoined his friend who shook his head knowingly at Ridley's passion. "Best not to let the volume of your complaints meet the level of your preaching." He wrinkled his nose. "But I will allow, it is awfully damp. And chilly, too. And yes, it seems the gentry and local lords take advantage of this space to talk freely. But this church is simple in its arrangement. And it is much better than imprisonment in the Tower of London. I am hopeful that our friend Latimer might be released soon."

"Simple is one thing," replied Ridley, thankful the scattered huddles of folk paid them no attention. "Dank and gloomy is another. Nature would do this place a favor if one day we had a great fire and it was rebuilt by a true master builder. For that matter, we could do the same to the Tower."

They both plodded silently along, matching their pace as they moved toward the altar. Cranmer was content to allow Ridley to speak his thoughts first, and to speak at length when he knew the words to impart would be most penetrating and practical. He was that way with friends as he was with those he met for the first time.

"The king has indeed allowed it to fall into some level of disrepair," he said, "but given he has other concerns of late, not to mention his grievous health, one can understand. We'll go beyond the altar to the sacristy. We should have private speaking quarters there."

"Bishop Bonner won't interject himself?" asked Ridley, looking around to see if they were being watched.

"His Grace was in Gloucester yesterday, desiring to be at the ordination of a cousin," Cranmer shrugged. "I made arrangements with the cathedral dean if we could meet here, for which I am glad you were on time. I have some serious matters to discuss with you."

"Thomas," said Ridley, who appreciated the archbishop's desire to be addressed by him on first-name terms, "almost everything you say is serious, for which I am thankful in these uncertain days."

Cranmer opened a door at the back of the sanctuary. "This way," he beckoned.

"The king's failing health is less slow decline than a sharp drop," Ridley agreed. "And if Edward is to be king afterward, our hopes are not necessarily secured."

Cranmer folded his hands, exhaling slowly. "I do not expect him to live past tomorrow. And upon his death, we will need the grace of the Holy Spirit to nurture a nine-year-old king for the calling that Almighty God will see fit to place upon his shoulders and the crown that Christ places on his head. We have borne heavy loads to come to this moment. Now we must look to the future."

"And to what end do you require our help?" asked Ridley.

"I have summoned you because I trust you with all my heart," said Cranmer. "First, we must speak about our friend Hugh. I understand why Latimer has refused to retake his bishop's role, even if he is freed upon the king's death. Whether he is or not, I would ask you remain close at hand for what lies ahead, Nicholas. I am appointing you to be the new Bishop of Rochester. I know you have enjoyed the teaching life at Pembroke, but like the colt on Palm Sunday, the Lord has need of you. I have need of you to be closer."

"And why do I sense you have more for me to do than just change my scenery?" Ridley pressed.

Cranmer laid his palms on the table before continuing. "We have plodded slowly, advancing the Gospel as evangelical allies here in England while King Henry lives. Although he threw off the yoke of the pope, it never meant he truly loved the free gift of the Gospel of Christ, the pure preaching of the Word, as we do. So, I have had to mark progress by small steps, but in the meanwhile I have been privileged to tutor the heir to the throne in Scripture within our reforming measures. Edward is certain to be our ally, even as others assist him, and so we shall muster our gifts to Christ's glory. Nicholas, I need you to collaborate with me, to help me compile our beliefs, our worship, the very way we approach Almighty God, so that our nation might speak with one voice as we praise Christ together and seek His face."

"A common worship?" Ridley inquired.

"Yes, a book that will lay the feast of our common prayer that we might bring before our Lord. I will need your help. I can write as the Lord leads, but you have the gift of organizing and editing."

"And what else?"

"I am also compiling a number of sermons to be bound together. If you are to be a bishop, I will need you to ensure the distribution of these sermons to the churches in your diocese."[1]

"Why, Thomas, if we expect all our priests to be able to preach according to Scripture?"

---

1. A diocese is a geographical region of churches in the Church of England. A bishop would be the leader of a diocese, responsible to oversee and guide the priests of the individual churches.

"They *should* be able to preach, Nicholas. Not every priest can preach well. And until their ability matches their calling to ministry, these sermons—which they can read out loud to their congregations—will ensure that Scripture is proclaimed with the glory and clarity our Lord deserves."

"So, a book of common prayer and a book of homilies[2], then?" Ridley looked at the fine, colorful vestments of Bishop Bonner's hanging in the sacristy. "To think of where we were just fifteen years ago, Thomas! Who could have imagined God would bring us to today?"

"God Himself, that is certain," Cranmer remarked. "Think about the days when we were so joyous for the free grace of Christ re-discovered, when Bilney and Latimer led those sessions from the White Horse Inn over dinner. And then when we had that dreadful stretch when the king asked to annul his marriage."

"King Henry has been helpful to us, Thomas. But I do nonetheless pray for his soul. He has been such a calculating man, giving us a wide berth to minister, yet it seems every other year he has a new bride."

"I am not saying it has been easy, Nicholas. But I do believe we have been slowly finding more light shining upon the Church in our land. Remember, just eight years ago, the king called me to his court and declared his newfound desire that an English Bible be placed in every church in our nation. Who would have believed that years before?"

"I would scarcely have believed it now," laughed Ridley. "The Bible that the king had William Tyndale burned for, the same Tyndale who at his death pleaded that God open the king's eyes."

"I would say that God did just that. And it is encouraging that Tyndale's death was one that bore that sort of fruit."

2. A homily is another name for a sermon. The word *homiletics* is the practice of preparing and giving sermons.

Ridley looked pensive as they walked out of the sacristy into the heart of the cathedral, with many of the previously gathered having left. "I wonder if we will have blessed days ahead, or if the storm clouds will gather and our lives will be hunted. What do you think, Thomas?"

Cranmer rubbed his cheek, his fingers scraping over the gathering stubble that now adorned his normally smooth visage. "Even if our lives are under threat by the executioner's blade or by the fiery stake, they are blessed, Nicholas. I am hopeful of days ahead in which our faith and reforming efforts flourish beyond our most vivid dreams. I look at what I intend to happen under the young Edward, and I wonder if our Lord Christ has so arranged these events so we might be part of building His kingdom in such robust fashion here in England, as Luther in Germany, as Calvin in Geneva. I am in constant correspondence with Calvin, with Bucer, with Melanchthon, and I dream of the day for a great union of our efforts together, a family gathering, only we are seeing our spiritual brothers for the first time! All this I hope for and at times I believe it is truly in our grasp." He looked up as they approached the great doors at the west portico. "And yet I remember how difficult it has been to establish the Gospel afresh in this land. All that could be swept away given the wrong leader, the wrong circumstances. We could suffer and die in savage manner. But Christ is our Lord, and He suffered on our accounts beyond our imagination. Whatever comes, it is to Him we must be faithful."

"We have been forced to take the slow path of reform, Thomas," Ridley said as they exited the church together, walking toward Warwick Lane. "But I am glad we had a steady hand in you to see us through. Very well! I accept your summons to go to Rochester! It will put me closer to helping you in time of need. And if Hugh is released from the Tower soon, perhaps God will see fit to shine the light of His grace in England through us. A small band to be sure, but Christ has conquered with small bands of allies before."

"And there are more who hope for our success here, Nicholas," Cranmer answered. "We are never without hope. Now, I must leave for Whitehall. I can only pray the king will still be alive when I enter his quarters."

With a heavy heart, Cranmer sat at the king's bedside, watching his monarch sleep fitfully, his chest rising and falling in uneven breaths. Cranmer himself had not slept at all, content to sit in the chair provided by the royal household, his eyes rarely leaving the king's dying form except to read from the Scriptures in his lap.

The door behind him creaked open, and Cranmer heard the footsteps approach to his right. Turning his head, he saw William Paulet, who had let him in to the palace just eight hours before. Paulet, the Lord Steward of the Royal Household, gazed blearily upon the king before turning to Cranmer.

"Is there anything I might have brought up from the palace kitchen for you, Archbishop?" he asked. "You have the look of a man who desperately needs his strength."

"If you please, my lord," Cranmer replied, "I would prefer to see him through to the end before I eat. But I thank you for your kind offer."

"I merely offered what we have. Sir Anthony Denny here was the true hero, sending the message for you to come with all speed."

Cranmer nodded at Sir Anthony, seated silently at the base of the bed near an assortment of pans, tears splashing his cheeks.

"Archbishop," said Paulet, "it would help if you speak with the king, even though he cannot respond. His Majesty was most anxious that you come for his peace."

"His peace?" asked Cranmer.

"He believes he shall have none after he passes," Sir Anthony spoke in rasps, "for he knows he has not lived a life of good deeds."

Cranmer rose from his chair and approached the bed. "Then he can take heart from the thief crucified to the right of our Lord Christ. He entered Paradise even though his sins far outweighed his blessed deeds." He sat on the bed, looking down at the suffering and bloated frame of the king who had given him position and privilege. Now Cranmer had come to urge his monarch to one last hope.

"My king," he whispered, "Your Majesty."

Perhaps the king was not in a deep slumber; perhaps he recognized the voice of his great churchman. Whatever the reason, Henry's eyes fluttered open to see Cranmer's stubbled face above his own, and the archbishop's eyes were shining.

"My king," Cranmer said as the door opened across the room, and Queen Catherine entered, raising her hand peaceably. "O King, I have come as you requested."

King Henry, with all the strength he could marshal, flopped his right hand toward Cranmer, palm up, and the archbishop clasped it.

"Your Majesty," Cranmer began, "I do not expect a sound from you. I know your illness has robbed you of your speech. But the King of heaven knows your limitations and will listen in any way you can make plain. Yet hear me this once."

The king's throat gurgled. The queen sat on the other side of the bed and stroked her husband forehead.

Cranmer began. "As with my own, I am aware of your sins, and you would not have summoned me if they were not known to you. I simply tell you that you are one of the many. St. Paul himself told the Roman Christians that indeed 'All have offended, and fall far short of the glory of God.' That, my lord, is the misery that enshrouds us all, from which we cannot work escape. And yet, I would plead for you to see that brings the most glorious news from heaven, for the same apostle tells us in the next breath that 'we are justified freely by His grace, by the redemption which is in Jesus Christ, Whom God has presented to us as a reconciler and peacemaker, through faith in His blood, to show His righteousness.' O my King, that righteousness can be yours this hour before you depart this earth!"

Henry hacked and winced, the pain from his ulcerated wounds draining life from him. He looked at his wife, then to Cranmer, on whom he fixed a desperate, pleading look. Cranmer knew time was critical.

"My good King Henry," he continued, "do not despair because of your lack of good. There is nothing on our part that will raise us to God's blessed love and acceptance, only a true faith, a lively faith, His gift to you, if you will receive Him! Run from His grace no longer, my lord. Receive Christ, and rest in Him!"

The queen and others present were weeping openly now. Cranmer placed the king's hand between both of his own and went on.

"Call on Christ and plead His mercy, my king," he sighed. "Though you cannot speak to plead with our Savior, give some token you are throwing yourself upon His glorious and kind self, awash in the riches of His grace! Open your eyes as wide as you can, or better yet—take your hand and press it against mine, that you do fully and completely lay your trust upon our blessed Jesus, whose blood covers all your sin and will be your righteousness!"

So faint was Henry's touch that Cranmer thought he had already passed, but in the next moment, Cranmer saw the royal fingers budge, then curve, wringing his hand with all the strength he could collect! The king and archbishop locked eyes one last time. No words. No elaborate anointing or ritual. Only a grip of a hand that mirrored the grip of Christ on the soul of the king.

"He is still," came the voice of the Lord Steward behind Cranmer.

"He is at peace," Cranmer wept. "My greatest struggle thus far is done, for my greatest prayer is finally answered by my God."

The English reformer **THOMAS CRANMER** (1489-1556) was appointed as the Archbishop of Canterbury during a tumultuous time in the Church of England. Navigating the church through the messy waters of King Henry VIII's marriages and carefully implementing the truths of the sufficiency of grace, faith, Christ, and Scripture, Cranmer sought to transform what became the Anglican Church into a robust Protestant community. His authorship of the Book of Common Prayer, much of the Book of Homilies, and what became known as the 'Thirty-Nine Articles of Religion', left an imprint on English religion and the English language for years to come. Though he recanted under torture during the reign of Mary I, he took back his words and affirmed his Protestant faith before being burned to death on March 21, 1556, in Oxford. Above all, his greatest legacy might have been his abiding belief that the grace of Christ abounds so greatly that no one is beyond repentance and being caught in the embrace of the God of love.

FACT FILES

Martyrs of the Reformation

One of the most serious reminders Jesus gave His disciples came the night before His death. In the Upper Room, Jesus told them of a darkness that would pursue His friends because of their allegiance to Him. He said:

> *"If the world hates you, know that it has hated me before it hated you. If you were of the world, the world would love you as its own; but because you are not of the world, but I chose you out of the world, therefore the world hates you"* (John 15:18-19).

And He even goes on to tell them why this hatred will manifest itself in brutality and death:

> *"I have said all these things to you to keep you from falling away. They will put you out of the synagogues. Indeed, the hour is coming when whoever kills you will think he is offering service to God" (John 16:1-2).*

Persecution and affliction for followers of Jesus is nothing new. Even before the Reformation, Christians who desired a return to the Scriptures and faith alone in Christ faced danger and death. The hunted Waldensians and the Bohemian pastor John Hus were such examples (refer to the previous volume in this series, *Reign*). Protestant martyrs detailed in chapters within this book are Patrick Hamilton, William Tyndale, Thomas Cranmer, and Lady Jane Grey. In fact, we are seeing increasing trials for those who are loyal to Christ.[1] And while the Protestant Reformation

1. And to be entirely fair, there is persecution against many non-Christian minorities, such as shown historically in the Holocaust against Jews and today as the Chinese Communist government practices torture and genocide against the Uyghur Muslim minority in the Xinjang region.

illumined the centrality of Scripture, Christ, grace, and faith, it saw stretches when its adherents were subject to horrific devastation and death. While their persecutors might have believed their work would stamp out the Protestant faith, it had the opposite effect, demonstrating that the ancient church leader Tertullian spoke rightly when he said, "The blood of the martyrs is the seed of the church." There were many who gave their life for the Reformation faith; a few examples are given here.

Jan Van Essen and *Hendrik Vos* are not considered major contributors to Reformation teaching, but their resolve and determination earned them a place as the first Lutheran martyrs of the Reformation. Like Luther, they participated as monks in an Augustinian monastery. While Luther's was in Germany, Van Essen and Vos dwelt in Antwerp (in modern-day Belgium) at St. Augustine's monastery. While there, all the monks became convicted by Luther's teachings that spread from Wittenberg. In 1522, a local bishop had the monks imprisoned in Vilvoorde (where William Tyndale was imprisoned and condemned) and threatened with burning. All but three of the monks turned away from their beliefs and returned to Catholicism. Those three were Van Essen, Vos, and their friend Lampertus Thorn (he would die in prison). Even under intense questioning, none of them recanted their beliefs, and on July 1, 1523, Van Essen and Vos were taken to the central market in Brussels, tied to the stake, and burned alive.

Although Luther, Calvin, and Cranmer are among the familiar Reformation names, we would do well to remember a group of reformers who wanted to take things further. The Anabaptist movement of the Swiss Brethren appreciated many of Ulrich Zwingli's reforms in Zurich in the 1520s, but Anabaptist theologians such as *Balthasar Hubmaier* did not believe they had gone in a fully Scriptural direction. Hubmaier, along with other Anabaptists, taught that baptism should be reserved for people who were making a profession of faith in Jesus Christ and should not be done for infants who could make no such profession. Hubmaier also believed in a more distinct separation between the church and the civil government, whereas with Zwingli there were more connections between the two. There were several public disputations between Zwingli and Hubmaier, which resulted in Hubmaier leaving Zurich for Nikolsburg in Moravia (now the Czech Republic). There, his preaching won over many converts, but attracted the hostile attention of Holy Roman Emperor Ferdinand I, who had become king of the region. Ferdinand had Hubmaier and his wife arrested and brought to Vienna, where they were tried and condemned. Hubmaier was burned to death on March 10, 1528, with his wife Elisabeth urging him to be faithful to the bitter end. Three days later, soldiers tied a stone around her neck and drowned her in the Danube River.

While Patrick Hamilton is known as the original Scottish Reformation martyr, *George Wishart* was also executed in St. Andrews in like manner as Hamilton. Wishart was a careful and well-respected schoolmaster and Bible teacher in the Scottish town of Montrose, and afterward he was a traveling preacher in other places like Dundee, Ayr, Perth, Edinburgh, and others, with John Knox as his bodyguard. Wishart translated the first confession of faith of the Swiss Reformers into English, and he spoke out boldly against the errors of the Roman papacy and the spiritual errors of the Church at large. In the end, Archbishop Beaton (who had condemned Hamilton) had Wishart arrested at Ormiston in southeastern Scotland. Beaton held a heresy trial against Wishart at St. Andrews Cathedral, but Wishart's skillful and gracious responses from Scripture brought on such sympathy from the nobles in attendance that Beaton cleared the cathedral before condemning Wishart to death. Almost eighteen years to the day following Hamilton's death, Wishart was burned at the stake. His death paved the way for John Knox's eventual leadership of the Scottish Reformation and hardened the Protestants against the Catholic authorities.

In 1553, Mary, daughter of Henry VIII and Catherine of Aragon, took the English throne (see the chapter on Lady Jane Grey) and re-instituted Catholicism throughout England. Known as "Bloody Mary", she oversaw the execution of nearly three hundred Protestant martyrs throughout her brief five-year reign. While Archbishop Thomas Cranmer is known for his martyrdom during this time, he also suffered the loss of his fellow Reformers and dear friends *Hugh Latimer* and *Nicholas Ridley.* Latimer had served as a bishop in Worcester and also as chaplain to King Edward VI, guiding him to a deeper allegiance to the Protestant faith. Ridley was the bishop of London and a skilled and dedicated preacher. The accession of the Catholic Mary to the English throne placed Cranmer, Latimer, and Ridley in grave danger, but they refused to flee the country. Arrested, they languished in prison for many months, encouraging each other with Scripture and prayer. Finally, Latimer and Ridley were brought to a trial in which the verdict was practically an afterthought. Condemned to death for heresy, Latimer and Ridley were taken on October 16, 1555, to a ditch near Baliol College in Oxford, where a pyre of wood and straw was readied for their execution; Cranmer was forced to watch the proceedings from a nearby tower. After the binding ropes were tied tightly, the officers placed a lit torch at their feet. As the flames climbed higher, Latimer called out, "Be of good cheer, brother Ridley, and **play the man!** We shall this day light such a candle by God's grace in England, as I trust shall never be put out!"

The suffering of faithful believers was not limited to men and theologians in major places. We find the inspiring stories of ordinary women in remote places who were determined to be faithful to the end. On the island of Guernsey, in the English Channel, the sisters *Guillemine Gilbert* and *Perotine Massey* lived in a house together with their mother *Katherine Cawches.* Perotine's husband was a French minister who favored the theology of John Calvin; he was in London at the time. During Mary's rule in 1556, the women were summoned to court on a charge that they had received a fellow citizen's stolen goblet. They were declared innocent of this charge, but in the course of that trial, evidence emerged of their Protestant beliefs. Imprisoned quickly at Castle Rock, they were re-tried at St. Peter's Church in Guernsey, this time for heresy. Condemned to death, the Royal Court ordered them executed on July 18th. All three women were burned alive together, and a tragic addition to this utterly sad moment is that Perotine was pregnant, and her child perished, as well.

Space does not permit us to tell the stories of all the martyrs who gave their lives as a witness to the Gospel of Jesus Christ, but that does not detract from their faithfulness to Him, nor does the suffering of those who perish for their faith mean they have been abandoned by God! Quite the opposite, if we trust the words of the apostle Paul (who knew a thing or two about suffering and martyrdom) at the end of Romans 8:

> *"Who shall separate us from the love of Christ? Shall tribulation, or distress, or persecution, or famine, or nakedness, or danger, or sword? As it is written, 'For your sake we are being killed all the day long; we are regarded as sheep to be slaughtered.'*
>
> *No, in all these things we are more than conquerors through him who loved us. For I am sure that neither death*

nor life, nor angels nor rulers, nor things present nor things to come, nor powers, nor height nor depth, nor anything else in all creation, will be able to separate us from the love of God in Christ Jesus our Lord!"
(Romans 8:35-39)

LADY JANE GREY

July 1553-February 1554

The flickering candlelight made the ascent up the stairwell rather treacherous. Fortunately for young Jane, the journey over rain-slickened roads to arrive at Greenwich Palace had been even more harrowing, and so she had no fear as she took one step after another, drawing closer to the chamber room. Her heart pounded, though, for other reasons. *Why have I been summoned?* She wondered. Jane and her husband Guildford had been enjoying a brief stroll in Shepherd's Bush Green, fragrant with the morning's rain, when the rider had pulled up and given his plea.

"My lady," he pleaded, "please enter this carriage at once. Your father the Duke of Suffolk, as well as you father-in-law the Duke of Northumberland[1], both demand your presence."

Jane hesitated, a brief lull that allowed Guildford to inquire first. "Does the king call for both of us?"

The rider shook his head. "He didn't mention you, m'lord. Word has been given to procure Lady Jane. Her presence is sorely needed."

"His Majesty the King being gravely ill is all we know," Guildford pressed. "Why do the dukes need to see my wife and not myself also?"

"Peace, Guildford," Jane said quietly, embarrassed by the pleading of her husband.

---

1. Lady Jane Grey's father, Henry Grey, was the Duke of Suffolk, and her father-in-law, John Dudley, was the Duke of Northumberland. They were members of King Edward VI's Privy Council that enforced Edward's change in the succession act that cleared the way for Jane—rather than Edward's half-sisters Mary or Elizabeth—to become monarch after his death.

"I have every right to ask," Guildford put in.

"M'Lord, the dukes gave no reason," said the rider, "and their desires are not to be questioned but speedily obeyed." He turned to Lady Jane as the carriage drew up next to them. "M'lady? Your transport."

They had pulled away leaving Guildford with a pained look on his face, but it was nowhere near the sadness Jane felt when the page opened the door to the chamber room where her father and father-in-law stood. Even before they said a word, Jane could sense a weight of grief and difficult news. Walking to her father, she kissed him on the cheek before turning to John Dudley and granting the same gesture to her father-in-law.

"Dear father," she said, with hands clasped lightly in front of her, "what might be the purpose of this summons?"

Placing his hand tenderly on her shoulder, Henry Grey took a deep breath. "We have summoned you here for a very serious matter, a result of the events of three days ago, events which have not been made public."

Looking at the Duke of Northumberland and then back at her own father, Jane felt her heart beginning to pound. "And what might that be?" she asked, although she knew deep within her bones what her father would say.

Henry Grey swallowed hard. "Your cousin, King Edward, died three days ago on the sixth." He put up a hand as if he could stem the pooling of tears in his daughter's eyes. "I am sorry we did not inform you at the moment, but please trust us as we had our reasons."

Jane took a kerchief and dabbed her eyes. The sorrow she felt was blunted by her thanks that Edward's suffering was over. He had been prone on his bed and coughing furiously, his lungs quickly giving out. The young ruler, not sixteen years of age yet, had been frail and sickly the last time Jane had visited him, with sweat pouring off his forehead as he twitched horribly.

"Then," Jane asked both men, "for what reason have you summoned me, if it relates to the king's death?"

"That is the question that much of London would ask if they saw you arrive," the Duke of Northumberland sputtered. "The truth is you are here so we might offer you the throne."

There it is, thought Jane, knowing there was much more these men had not yet shared with her. *Surely either Mary or Elizabeth is the natural choice,* she thought, *although I pray it would not be Mary lest we return to the darkness of years past.*

"My lords," she said, as calmly as she could, "why have I been named the successor?"

Her father breathed deeply again. His eyes watering, he blinked and looked adoringly at Jane. "Because, dear Jane, it involves you. It will involve our blessed nation of England in a great crisis that is needed to prevent an entirely worse crisis from occurring."

"I'm not sure I follow your logic, dear father," Jane pleaded.

"Edward chose you, dearest one," Lord Grey began, "because he could not bear the thought of England demolished under an ocean wave of Catholic resurgence after his death. If Mary was named queen, that is what would occur. And then all we have fought for ... the establishment of true religion under Archbishop Cranmer, the hope we have of salvation in Christ by His grace—not by works—as declared by our evangelical faith ... all that would come down like a house of dry sticks!"

"But Mary was his eldest sister," Jane reminded him.

"Of that he was well aware," Northumberland replied, "just as Elizabeth was born prior to Edward, and as he left behind no male heir at only sixteen years of age, what shall be done? It does revert to Mary. But this cannot be. Our religion will be crushed under her."

"Then what about Elizabeth?"

Jane's father ran his fingers through his hair and put out his hand. "She is unmarried, and what if that continues? If she continues so as queen, she will bring about no heirs, let alone male heirs." He paused. "It is a technical matter, and although I would be more confident in her religion than Mary's, there is one in whom Edward had supreme confidence in her faith." He paused again. "And in an ability to produce a male line of heirs if needed, for that person is married."

"You're speaking of me?" Jane exclaimed, understanding where this conversation was leading.

"Yes," the king responded. "This person in question was married just five weeks ago. To Guildford, my son."

The weight of the moment came down heavily upon young Jane. "You are asking me to succeed the king?" She did not want the throne, and the marriage with Guildford was already producing enough trials, but there was something about their request that she could not turn from.

"You have placed your faith in the Lord Jesus Christ alone for salvation from your sins," her father replied, "and you hold to Christ alone by faith alone and derive your hope from Scripture alone so that by grace alone your sole desire is to live for the glory of Almighty God. No, dear Jane, we are not merely asking you to sit on the throne. Edward named you to be queen after him. He did so by officially changing the line of succession, with the understanding of the entire Privy Council, including us."

Taking a step closer, the Duke of Northumberland extended a rolled-up document toward Jane. "The late king's Device of Succession," he said, "dictated and signed by him, if there be any dispute. Receive your holy summons, dearest Jane. And may God be with you."

Jane, mouth open, could not believe what she had heard. So lost in her thoughts was she that their voices seemed far away. But then her father placed his hand on her shoulder again and asked, a pleading tone in his voice

"Dearest Jane," he whispered, "how do you not know that you have been given this opportunity for such a time as this?"

Jane stood resolute in the flickering candlelight, but the place was different. Her room was no longer in Greenwich Palace. There was no king. Edward had died the day after he proclaimed Jane would succeed him. And now she was no longer Queen of England. Mary's sudden invasion had brought Jane's brief reign to a crushing halt after less than two weeks. The candle illumined the prison cell, allowing Jane to see the few books she was allowed within the Tower of London, but little else. And she could not see dearest Guildford, who was imprisoned elsewhere in the labyrinth of rooms.

The iron door scraped over the stony floor as Humphrey, the guard, stepped into the cell, holding a bowl of gruel in his hand. His face, stern at first, softened when he saw Jane standing dignified before him.

"Begging pardon, m'lady," he uttered, bowing slightly, "but I nearly failed to deliver your food and a notice." He nodded for her to move from the door while he set the bowl and spoon upon the low table under the barred window.

"It is nothing for which you must beg forgiveness," Jane replied kindly. "It has given me much happiness to hear your voice, Humphrey." She lingered by the far wall. "You do have an interesting accent, good sir. When you say *pardon*, I hear *pair-den*, and failed becomes *faye-eld*."

Humphrey stood straight in addressing Jane. "That be m' Cumbrian accent, m'lady. Although I've found my way to London to originally serve in th' army, I was born in a small village there—Appleby by name—where m'father was a baker."

"Well, to me, it's a lovely accent, good Humphrey, and I am glad you've not lost it. But you also said you bore a notice?"

And here Humphrey looked very grave. "I do, m'lady. Her Majesty's chaplain, Feckenham, has arrived and desires an audience."

"With me?"

Humphrey nodded.

"Here?"

"Yes, m'lady. He has come with her palace guard. Two of them will accompany him into this cell, if you will." He bowed once more and backed out through the door.

Christ will be with me. My Shepherd will guide me.

Jane opened her eyes, looking up from her kneeling position and beheld John Feckenham positioned before her. The chaplain stood just inside the doorway, his thick brown hair swept across his head while his beard looked as if he hadn't trimmed it since Christmas. Clad in a white robe and black hooded cloak, Feckenham's eyes gazed upon Jane with kindness. Although he was the queen's chaplain, Jane knew Feckenham would listen to her and desired the best for her. Mary had chosen him well. She was popular with many people, and Mary did not gain that high regard by being cruel but rather by surrounding herself with the right people.

Brushing a wart on his left index finger, the chaplain's eyes looked over his hands directly at Jane.

"Good lady," he spoke, his voice calm, "I have come to make you an offer by which you might live."

"Why do you call me good, O Feckenham, when only God is good? You say this when I am condemned to die tomorrow. I do not doubt your heart, kind sir, but why have you come to my cell? Many of the queen's enemies have been crushed, with only my father and myself to eliminate. Why would there even be an offer?"

Feckenham gulped and nodded. Gesturing to the guards to stay outside the cell, he placed a stool next to Jane and took his chained cross in his hands, turning it over and over. "Oh, Jane, Jane, Jane," he muttered. "So fierce and determined even up to death's door. After the rebellion of your allies, the surrender and treason of your father-in-law, every breath you expend here in this cell is a gift. The queen's gift."

"The gift is from God, O Feckenham," Jane said softly but firmly. "That, in fact, is what makes it grace."

"Your plunge into the things of Almighty God is noble, dear lady," Feckenham sighed, leaning forward from his seat. "It is overwhelming to think that you, at your age, could be well versed in the truth of religion."

"You do recall," replied Jane, "that the Apostle Paul implored the youthful Timothy to stand firm in his faith. And when he did, he told Timothy not to let anyone look down upon his because of his tender age."

Feckenham smiled, amazed at Jane's wisdom and charity even though the chasm of religious allegiance between them was too wide. "I have to admit, my lady," he said, "that I cannot help but be impressed by the depth of your insight. But I would beg you, as a fellow citizen, as a friend, to take this path out of your cell: Turn from your confusion and the spell under which the late King Edward placed you. Return to the true religion of the holy apostles and the merits of the saints who can lift you up in grace before Christ Himself!" Standing up, he extended his hand, he continued, "If you will but kiss my hand as a token that you will return to the Church of Rome, the church invigorated by the glory of God, then even now you can be spared."

Jane bowed her head. *All I have sought in my short life is to please Christ,* she thought. *And now it appears I can best serve Him through my death.*

Looking up at the chaplain, Jane shook her head firmly. "No, Feckenham. In this vale of sadness, I am comforted by your compassion for me and your friendship with me. But as to the saints whom you claim can lift me up in grace before my Lord, I have this reply: I am saved from death and hell by grace alone, in Christ alone, through faith alone. And you shall not take me from that firm ground."

Feckenham's lips quivered, but his words were controlled. "Then you know what this means, dear lady," he said, a tear sliding from his eye. "In three days' time, you shall go to the firm ground of Tower Green to meet your end."

"I know," said Jane, her own voice placid. "I only ask one request, that you be there with me."

Feckenham laid his hand on her arm, squeezing it lightly. "That I can do."

The chilly wind swirled through Tower Green as Jane stepped tremulously across the grass. A small crowd watched her approach the center of the green silently, breathing heavily. Whether it was from the cold or because of her coming death, none could say. But Jane knew. In a few minutes, she reasoned calmly, I will be in my Savior's arms.

Looking around for Queen Mary, Jane could not locate her, but she imagined her cousin was either watching from a distance or waiting to receive news of Jane's demise. She saw Feckenham draw abreast of her, his scraggly beard fluttering in the stiff breeze. "I have prayed for you, my child," he said, choking back the tears.

"And I for you," Jane replied, "and I am thankful for your kindness in my final days. I will leave this life counting you as a friend."

He nodded. "And I, you." He swallowed painfully. "Come," he said, gesturing toward the chopping block. "And if you wish to say a few words to the gathering today, you have that right." He put his mouth to her ear and whispered gently. "As a queen."

Jane smiled and hugged him tightly, then turned to the assembly. *Be Christ to them*, she thought, *for they must see the Lord in your dying.*

"My lords," she began, "and you good Christian people, who come to see me die: I am condemned to die, not for offending the Queen's Majesty. My hands are clean of that charge, and I deliver to my God a soul pure and innocent of that injustice." Jane paused, crossing her hands over her breast. "However,

I know I have offended Almighty God when I pursued my desires and pleasures of this wretched world, preferring my pride and rebellion above the grace that God has given me. And so, I thank Him with all my heart that He granted me time to repent of my sins here in this world, and to reconcile myself to my Redeemer, Jesus Christ my Lord. My lords, and all you good Christian people, I must earnestly desire you all to pray with and for me while I am still alive. Pray that God of His infinite goodness and mercy will forgive me my countless sins against Him, and I beg you all to bear witness of this: Here I will die as a true Christian woman, pledging from my soul's depths that I trust to be saved by the blood and death of my crucified Savior, Jesus Christ alone, and by no other means."

Closing her eyes and reopening them, Jane smiled, the joy in her heart cascading through her body. "This day I cast away every attempt of mine to gain eternal life on my own, and instead I cast myself into the nail-scarred hands of my Risen King." She walked toward the block. "And now, I pray you all pray for me, and with me."

LADY JANE GREY, whose reign as Queen of England lasted a mere nine days in July 1553, stood firm in her Protestant faith during a difficult time. Dedicating herself to the teachings of the Reformation, she was chosen by her dying cousin, King Edward VI, to be queen after his death. This selection set off a crisis in which Mary, Edward's oldest half-sister, rallied her supporters to gain the crown and began making England a Catholic nation again. A rebellion on Jane's behalf failed, and Mary finally condemned her to death by beheading on February 12, 1554. Her loving spirit, hunger for the Bible, and her determined faith in Jesus make her a model of Christian action in the deepest of trials.

JOHN KNOX

June 24, 1563; Holyrood Palace, Edinburgh, Scotland

"Minister! Minister Knox!" the shout went up from the east, and the bearded pastor straightened himself as he took labored steps up Canongate Street, the palace coming into full view. Seeing his friend Lord Ochiltree running at full pelt toward him, John Knox raised his hand in acknowledgement and caution, as if the upward lift of his fingers could slow Ochiltree's reckless sprint.

"Slow yourself!" Knox called back as his friend and father-in-law approached and slowed his gallop to a trot. "The river has not overflowed its banks. Nobody has died. The English have not invaded across the border. Please tell me your concern as calmly as possible."

The lord stopped in front of Knox, oblivious to the bystanders who watched him desperately regain his breath with a series of initial heaves. "Not a flood of water, sir, but a flood of hostility. The palace guards announced that you are to be standing before the queen at half past the hour for your disputation with Her Majesty!"

"Her Majesty!" Knox scoffed, his voice betraying more frustration than he intended. Stroking his coarse beard, he nodded toward Holyrood Palace and beckoned Lord Ochiltree to come with him. "Do not fear the time of day, good sir. Rather, fear the Creator of time, for all of it is within the hollow of His hand. And half past the hour is no worry. I left the Kirk five minutes ago. That means another ten minutes of moderate pace, and we shall be at Holyrood. Come now."

His companion looked back to St. Giles, from where Knox had come, and saw threatening skies approaching overhead. "I wonder if the storms will come during your time with the queen. Here, Erskine is coming down the lane now. I think he has been granted privilege to enter with you."

"My time with Queen Mary will likely produce storms and quakes of its own, Andrew," Knox said chidingly, using his companion's first name. "Do not worry about the future, whether it is within arm's length or beyond many years. She has ordered me to come for a private meeting and so I will."

"For a private disputation?" asked Ochiltree. "I would not be so confident in that. Word is that she will have her provost and ladies-in-waiting in her throne chamber."

"Well, I am sure that is private enough for her," Knox joked, "and that grants me a larger number which might hear the instruction of Almighty God. Remember that large numbers do not guarantee that one holds to the truth. Stephen preached as one man against the entire Sanhedrin, and did so faithfully and boldly."

"He was killed, you know."

Knox suppressed a smile at the lord's rejoinder. "Which proves you know your Scripture, which is more than one can say for so many of the priests I've battled here in Scotland." He saw John Erskine approach them. "My friend, John. So good of you to come."

"I would not miss this for all the treasure in the world," smiled Erskine. "You shall have me here with you. I am afraid I am little use other than a reliable witness to the proceedings." He paused. "And for prayer."

"Prayer before our Redeemer is all we have in moments like these," said Knox. "I do want to thank you both sincerely, Andrew and John, in spite of my demeanor. Thank you for seeing me to Holyrood. Thank you for walking by my side on this journey."

"It is less than a mile, Minister Knox," Erskine noted.

"That wasn't the journey I was speaking of," Knox replied. "Ever since I raised consistent concerns with Mary over her return to our land, there have been fewer and fewer nobles and friends who remain with me in the fight to defend our Kirk. The alliance with France was spurned, and we have established the victory of our evangelical faith by our legitimized Confession!"

And then that woman returned a widow, taking the throne here when she should not. It was much to take in, but I wish I had more hands with me in the battle."

"I do not wish to blame you, sir," Lord Ochiltree responded gently, "but perhaps writing as you did against the governing authority by women might have been an arrow shot longer than our friends could make? It is not good you feel abandoned, but wasn't there much at stake?"

"Again, numbers do not win the battle. God wins the battle. And that is a matter on the borders of this disputation today. The queen intends to take a Catholic husband, and I—whether one believes I might be too forthright and graceless—will stand in the breach and declare what God gives me the right to declare. I do not seek to pour misery upon Mary's head, but to simply use my voice as a citizen of this land to call its rulers to account. We have that voice. I, as a minister of the Gospel, have that privilege and responsibility."

"A responsibility that you must marshal quickly," remarked Ochiltree as the gates of Holyrood rose in front of them. "May God give you grace in what you say."

"He will because He is the God of grace to sinners such as myself," Knox sighed, clasping Ochiltree's arm in farewell. "And I need not fear what words I must compile for this moment. I have the promise of Christ in Luke's Gospel: *When they bring you unto magistrates and powers, take no thought how or what thing you shall answer, for the Holy Spirit shall teach you in that same hour what to say.*"

Lord Ochiltree took a deep breath. "May He do so, my friend."

"He shall," Knox replied, turning toward the palace, "and He will always be ever faithful to you."

"This way," Erskine pointed toward the entry, "and let us have God do His work."

The flickering candles in the dark throne room made it appear as if ghosts danced on the walls. John Knox simply walked forward with an armed guard at his side, coming within twenty feet of the throne. There, with a stern look on her face, sitting bolt upright, was the Queen of Scotland. How many times had their words flown back and forth between the two of them, she the unyielding Catholic, he the resolute Protestant. *Once more into battle, Lord Jesus,* Knox prayed silently. *Please help me.*

Mary lifted her chin. She was of slighter frame than Knox, but sitting in her elevated position gave her a more dominating presence. Nodding to her provost, Robert Douglas, who nodded in turn to her ladies-in-waiting, she gave the call to order. Her ladies disappeared into the antechamber to the back.

"My most reverend subject, Master Knox," she began, "I am certain that you, like I, tire of these many growlings. You also must know that your place in this palace is afforded solely by my generosity."

"That is an odd statement," Knox replied upon her pause, "for I am led to believe by Holy Scripture that God is the one who grants time and place to us all."

"Sniveling rodent!" griped Douglas. "Keep your mouth shut until Her Majesty permits you to speak."

"I have said before that I see a woman who styles herself the Queen of Scotland, but *majesty* is a term I reserve for God, not her."

The provost took a step in Knox's direction, but Mary put out a hand. "Good sir, relent. Surely you can trust Master Knox and I to have a direct conversation?" Turning to Knox, she hardened her gaze. "My generosity exists despite my late mother's standing royal decree that outlawed your preaching four years ago, two years prior to my return to this throne! My willingness to invite you here is proof of my beneficial mercy."

"You have not invited me here, O Queen," Knox replied, slowly forcing out every word. "Your word to come was an inevitable summons. Here I am, though. May we speak plainly?"

"Speak plainly about your complaints against my rule and my faith?"

"You act as if any achievement I have brought to the Kirk in Scotland is a result of my grousing and morose complaints. I have plainly taught positive truths during my ministry here in Edinburgh and everywhere I've been since I was ordained at St. Andrews. I have spoken openly that Holy Scripture is the only and perfectly necessary standard of Christian faith. I have taught surely that we are justified and given right standing before God by faith in Jesus Christ alone. I have taught that—contrary to the ignorance and pride of the priests of your Church—true Christian ministers are simply gospel teachers, shepherds of the redeemed, and humble servants of all. And I have taught that the people have the right to elect those who minister to them—and a corollary to that is ministers have the right to question their rulers when they do wrong!"

"That was hardly the positive proclamation from your lips when you protested my return two years ago," Mary charged.

"I was protesting your celebration of the Roman Mass, O Queen," growled Knox, "in a nation that had chosen the evangelical faith of those who would reform against the abuses of Rome. Abuses that I know plenty about."

"Yes," interrupted the provost, "I think you put prayers to the Virgin Mary among those so-called abuses."

"An action I was told to undertake when a slave in the French galleys. It was in Nantes on the Loire that a captain brandished a picture of the Virgin Mary and ordered all of us to kiss it. When I refused, he pushed it into my face and I tore it from his hands, throwing it into the water."

"You heretic!"

"Then I'll tell you what I told him. '*Let our Lady now save herself: She is light enough, let her learn to swim!*'"

"Master Knox," Mary sighed deeply. "This avenue of remembrance is certainly helping us know your convictions in a clearer light, but it does not help us regarding why I have called you here today. Indeed, given your hatred of me, I would be surprised if we can have a civil conversation."

"O Queen, I have no hatred of you," Knox cautioned. "I can even admire your many good qualities. You are young and so you may be willing to learn. You are full of charm and high intelligence. But you are an enemy of all that the Kirk of Christ has fought for during the years of your absence. You are not the one to rule this land."

"A disdain that also cools any admiration my cousin Elizabeth might have for you," Mary retorted.

"England is England," said Knox, "and my concern is here. Particularly of my concern is your choice of marriage."

"The news of my private life reaching your ears saddens, but does not surprise me."

"O Queen, you have no private life," Knox implored. "Your life as it is lies bare before the public of this land."

Mary drew a couple of hardy breaths before responding. "Master Knox, am I never to be rid of you? You have openly criticized me, mocked my uncles in France, and even then, I have given you permission to tell me privately of my shortcomings, meeting with you whenever you felt you must berate me. In every way, I have attempted to be the reconciler. And yet you will never give me a moment's peace! So I swear to Him Who rules the world, I shall have justice and revenge!" Her eyes grew moist, and she dabbed them with a cloth, her body suddenly wracked with sobs.

Knox stood quietly by. He looked over at John Erskine and saw his head bowed in silent prayer. There was nothing to do but continue.

"Madam," he began, "we have had our clashes, you and I. But they will end when God delivers you from your prison of spiritual darkness and falsehood. I speak as Christ commands me to speak."

"Yes, but you are speaking against my proposed marriage to Don Carlos! To what end is that your right to weigh against me? What are you within this commonwealth of Scotland?"

"I am a subject born within the realm of Scotland, madam!" Knox shot back, causing Mary to flinch. "I may not be a lord, nor an earl, nor one of the barons who cautiously hedge between our Kirk and your own self for a greater advantage. However small and insignificant I may be in your sight, I am as worthy a member of this nation as anyone else." He looked at the queen, and her veil of tears pained his heart. "If this nation allows you to marry a husband unfaithful to Christ, then this nation will have spurned the rule of Christ."

"You are a cruel man to speak against my marriage!" Mary shrieked, the tears flowing quickly.

"One word, madam," said Knox, "and then you can banish me from this place, declare me unfit to stand in your presence, whatever your desire. I do not delight in anyone's tears. I can hardly endure the weeping of my own sons when I must discipline them, and much less can I rejoice in your sorrow. But I will bear your tears and lift up the truth of Christ, because any one has that calling to summon their monarch from disaster."

"Then leave, Master Knox," the queen snapped, "and never come to see me again!"

Knox nodded to the provost and then beckoned Erskine to come with him. At the door he stopped, turned to Mary, and gently said, "O Queen, you can cast me out to calm this storm between us, but if you continue in this, you will never quiet the storm in your heart. For you, I shall endeavor to pray." And with that, he was gone.

The Scottish Reformer **JOHN KNOX** lived a life of trouble, travel, and truth. Influenced greatly by Protestants like Patrick Hamilton and George Wishart in St. Andrews, Knox became a chaplain before being captured and enslaved on a French ship. Gaining his freedom, he eventually pastored a church in Newcastle, England, before studying further in Geneva under John Calvin and pastoring a church of English refugees in Frankfurt. Another stop at a church in Geneva preceded his return to Scotland, where his fiery preaching and bold leadership spearheaded the Reformation there. His written confession of faith, the Scots Confession, was adopted by the Scottish Parliament in Edinburgh, opening the way for Knox and others to organize the Reformed churches, or "Kirks" in Scotland. Knox's beliefs in elected government in the church led to representative government among the Presbyterian churches and his willingness to call out wrongdoing among leaders was a posture of other protest actions such as the civil rights movements.

WHERE WE GET OUR INFORMATION

Calvin, John. *Acts of the Council of Trent with Antidote.* https://www.monergism.com/thethreshold/sdg/calvin_trentantidote.html

Cardier, Jean. *The Man God Mastered.* Tr. From the French by O.R. Johnston. Grand Rapids: Eerdmans, 1960.

Calhoun, David. *In Their Own Words: The Testimonies of Martin Luther, John Calvin, John Knox, and John Bunyan.* Carlisle, PA: Banner of Truth Trust, 2018.

Collins, Chuck. *Cranmer's Church: Then and Today.* The Center for Reformation Anglicanism: Birmingham, AL, 2021.

D'Aubigne, Jean Henri Merle. *The Triumph of Truth: A Life of Martin Luther.* Tr. By Henry White. Edited by Mark Sidwell. Bob Jones University Press: Greenville, SC, 1996.

Durant, Will. *The Story of Civilization: The Reformation.* New York, NY: Simon & Schuster, 1957.

Edwards, Brian. *God's Outlaw: The Story of William Tyndale and the English Bible.* Evangelical Press: Darlington, UK, 1987.

Eells, Hastings. *Martin Bucer.* Yale University Press: New Haven, CT, 1931.

Estep, William. *The Anabaptist Story: An Introduction to Sixteenth-Century Anabaptism.* Eerdmans: Grand Rapids, MI, 1996.

Estep, William. *Renaissance and Reformation.* Eerdmans: Grand Rapids, MI, 1986.

Ferguson, Sinclair. *In the Year of our Lord: Reflections on Twenty Centuries of Church History.* Reformation Trust: Orlando, FL, 2018.

Foxe, John. *Foxe's Christian Martyrs of the World.* Barbour and Co.: Uhrichsville, OH, 1989.

Gatiss, Lee, ed. *The First Book of Homilies: The Church of England's Officials Sermons in Modern English.* Church Society/ Lost Coin Books: Watford, UK, 2021.

Gatiss, Lee. *Light After Darkness: How the Reformers Regained, Retold, and Relied on the Gospel of Grace.* Christian Focus Publications: Ross-shire, UK, 2019.

Gonzalez, Justo. *The Story of Christianity, vol. 2: From the Reformation to the Present Day.* New York, NY: Harper & Row, 1985.

Hsiu, R. Po-Chia, ed. *The Cambridge History of Christianity: Reform and Expansion, 1500-1660.* Cambridge, UK: Cambridge University Press, 2008.

Lawson, Steven J. *Pillars of Grace, A.D. 100-1564: A Long Line of Godly Men.* Ligonier Ministries: Orlando, FL, 2016.

Lempriere, Raoul. *History of the Channel Islands.* Robert Hale Ld., London, UK, 1974.

Littlejohn, Bradford and Jonathan Roberts, eds. *Reformation Theology: A Reader of Primary Sources with Introductions.* The Davenant Institute: Omaha, NE, 2018.

Loades, David. *Henry VIII and His Queens.* Sutton Publishing: Stroud, UK, 1994.

Loane, Sir Marcus. *Masters of the English Reformation.* Banner of Truth Trust: Edinburgh, UK, 2005.

MacCulloch, Diarmud. *Thomas Cranmer.* Yale University Press: New Haven, CT, 1996.

McGrath, Alister, ed. *The Christian Theology Reader, Third Edition.* Hoboken, NJ: Wiley-Blackwell, 2006.

Mueller, Janel M., ed. *Catherine Parr: Complete Works and Correspondence.* University of Chicago Press: Chicago, IL, 2014.

Moronici, Ambra. *Michelangelo's Poetry and Iconography in the Heart of the Reformation.* Routledge: Abingdon, UK, 2019.

Moynihan, Brian. *God's Bestseller: William Tyndale, Thomas More, and the Writing of the English Bible—A Story of Martyrdom and Betrayal.* St. Martin's Press: New York, NY, 2002.

Needham, Nick. *2000 Years of Christ's Power, Volume 3: Renaissance and Reformation.* Christian Focus Publications: Ross-shire, UK, 2016.

Null, Ashley and John W. Yates III, eds. *Reformation Anglicanism: A Vision for Today's Global Communion.* Crossway: Wheaton, IL, 2017.

Olson, Roger. *The Story of Christian Theology.* InterVarsity Press: Downers Grove, IL, 1999.

Parr, Queen Catherine. *The Lamentation of a Sinner.* Introduction by Don Matzat. Good News Books: O'Fallon, MO, 2017.

Selderhuis, H. J. *Marriage and Divorce in the Thought of Martin Bucer.* Thomas Jefferson University Press: Kirksville, MO, 1999.

Shelley, Bruce. *Church History in Plain Language.* Nashville, TN: Thomas Nelson, 1995.

Thompson, Bard. *Liturgies of the Western Church.* Fortress Press: Minneapolis, MN, 1980.

VanDoodewaard, Rebecca. *Reformation Women: Sixteenth Century Figures Who Shaped Christianity's Rebirth.* Reformation Heritage Books: Grand Rapids, MI, 2017.

Van Halsema, Thea B. *This Was John Calvin.* IDEA Ministries: Grand Rapids, MI, 1959.

Wallace, Robert. *The World of Leonardo: 1452-1519.* Time-Life Books: New York, NY, 1972.

Walton, Robert C. *Chronological and Background Charts of Church History.* Zondervan: Grand Rapids, MI, 1986.

Zwingli, Huldrych. *The Implementation of the Lord's Supper.* Tr. By Jim West. Pitts Theological Library: Atlanta, GA, 2016.

Zwingli, Ulrich. *Selected Works* [ed. by Samuel Macauley Jackson]. University of Pennsylvania Press: Philadelphia, PA, 1972.

EUROPE
SWEDEN
FINLAND
UK
HOLLAND
GERMANY
FRANCE
SWITZERLAND
ITALY

SCOTLAND
St Andrews
Edinburgh
The NETHERLANDS
BELGIUM
ENGLAND
Rotterdam
London
Antwerp
Guernsey
Strasbourg
FRANCE
Meux
Navarre

SWEDEN
FINLAND
NORWAY
TURKU
STOCKHOLM
DENMARK
WITTENBERG
GERMANY
MAINZ
WORMS

Vienna

SWITZERLAND

Zurich

AUSTRIA

Geneva

ITALY

Florence

Rome

Reign

The Church in the Middle Ages

Luke H. Davis

During the Middle Ages the church labored to build a community of faith. Benedict, Columba, and Francis organized communities in which the Gospel could be preached. Theodulf, Anselm, and Bernard of Clairvaux answered the call to reform that community and theology. And when the church's leaders drifted from the authority of Scripture, a first wave of reformers in Peter Waldo, John Wycliffe, and John Hus arose to call God's people back to the grace of God.

This was a Church that sought to reign, love and conquest, a Church that wanted to secure freedom, and proclaim the gospel. When that Church fell into corruption it undertook its own reform. Which one of these is the medieval Church? They all are! And in that we can find hope in the God Who loves His Church as we seek to live in His name.

ISBN: 978-1-5271-0801-1

Redemption

The Church in Ancient Times

Luke H. Davis

The story of the ancient Church is one of a people who were finding their way over many years by the light that God shined forth for them. Today, we are looking back over the centuries with many more years of understanding but we stand on the shoulders of those who braved persecution, death, debate, and mystery on behalf of generations to come. From the Apostle Peter at Pentecost in Jerusalem to St. Patrick on the shores of Ireland in the year 432 – the ancient church has much to teach the church of today.

Luke Davis has written a very accessible and enjoyable introduction to early church history. An ideal starting point for anyone's first plunge into those formative years of the church's life, faith, and worship.

Nick Needham

Lecturer in Church History, Highland Theological College, Dingwall, Scotland

ISBN: 978-1-5271-0801-1

Christian Focus Publications publishes books for adults and children under its four main imprints: Christian Focus, CF4K, Mentor and Christian Heritage. Our books reflect our conviction that God's Word is reliable and Jesus is the way to know him, and live for ever with him.

Our children's publication list covers pre-school to early teens. We also publish personal and family devotional titles, biographies and inspirational stories that children will love.

From pre-school board books to teenage apologetics, we have it covered!

Christian Focus Publications Ltd,
Geanies House, Fearn, Ross-shire,
IV20 1TW, Scotland,
United Kingdom.

Find us at our web page:
www.christianfocus.com